To Kill the Irishman

The War that Crippled the Mafia

Also by Rick Porrello

Superthief—A Master Burglar, the Mafia
and the Biggest Bank Heist in U.S. History

The Rise and Fall of the
Cleveland Mafia—Corn Sugar and Blood

TO
KILL
THE
IRISHMAN

THE WAR THAT CRIPPLED THE MAFIA

RICK PORRELLO

Next Hat

Press

Published by Next Hat Press
P.O. Box 23
Novelty, Ohio 44072
www.RickPorrello.com
Rick@RickPorrello.com

Distributed by BookMasters, Inc. 800-247-6553
Wholesalers include Ingram, Baker & Taylor,
Partners East, Partners West, and Brodart

(Retouched) Cover photo courtesy of WJW Television, Cleveland
Book Design by Frank DeMaio
Cover Design by Rick Porrello and Thomas Michael Basie
Printed by BookMasters, Inc.

Library of Congress Control Number 2004090634

Cataloging-in-Publication Data

Porrello, Rick
    To kill the Irishman: the war that crippled the Mafia / Rick Porrello.
        p. cm.
    Includes bibliographical references and index.
        ISBN 0-9662508-9-3   ISBN-13 978-0-9662508-9-3
    1. Greene, Danny.   2. Mafia—Ohio—Cleveland—History.   3. Organized
    Crime—United States.   4. Gangsters—Ohio—Cleveland—Biography. I. Title
HV6248.G74P67 1998
364.1092—dc21   2004090634
                                                                      CIP

Revised Edition, Sixth paperback printing.
(Tenth total printing)

Dedicated to Betty, Ray, Sue, Ray Jr.,

Lee and Christian

Acknowledgments

I would like to thank the following individuals and organizations for their contributions to this project.

Jim Ahearn, Akron, Ohio Police Department, Bakersfield, California Coroner's Office, Michael Bartone, Thomas Michael Basie, Lisa Beck, Tom Bird, Kimberly Bonvissuto, Tom Buford, California Office of the Attorney General, California Crime Commission, Lou Capasso, Bob Cermak, (Sister) Veronica Cipar, Cleveland Magazine, Cleveland Heights, Ohio Police Department, Cleveland, Ohio :Police Department, Cleveland, Ohio Police Museum, Cleveland State University (Cleveland Press Archives), (Judge) Donna Congeni-Fitzsimmons, Faith Corrigan, Vince Crawford, Cuyahoga County Common Pleas Court, Susan Daniels, Sandy Deak, Carl Delau, Peter DiGravio, Bob Dinsfriend, Peter Elliott (U.S. Marshals Service), (Sister) Barbara Eppich, Euclid, Ohio Police Department, Euclid Public Library, Federal Bureau of Investigation, Jim Fiore, (Judge) Norman A. Fuerst, Gary Garisek, Rich Gazarich, Lloyd Gladson, John Griffith, Ron Guenttzler, Dennis Gunsch, Richard T. Henshaw, Scott Hodes, John Carroll University, Emily Johnson, Wayne Kapantas, David Kerr, Lora Kong, Sue Kovach, Vic Kovacic, Dr. John Langer, Jim Litnar (Licavoli), Mike LoPresti, Mike Malone, Carmen Marino, Jim McCann, Nan McCarthy, Patricia Meade, Ann Millett, Moreland Hills, Ohio Police Department, National Military Personnel Records Center, Dennis Nicklas, Lisa Nussbaum, J. Kevin O'Brien, Doris O'Donnell-Beufait, Ohio Organized Crime Investigative Commission, Mike O'Mara, Bill Ouseley, Tony Paglia, Pat Parisi, Parmadale Catholic Home, Paul Patterson, Pennsylvania Crime Commission, Pennsylvania State Police—Bureau of Criminal Investigation, Dick Peery, Lennie Piazza, Joe Plisevich, Skip Ponikvar,

Lee Porrello, Ray Porrello, Rocco Poluttro, Dan Poynter, George Qua, Michael V. Renda, S.A. Reuscher, the late Bill Roemer, Tom & Marilyn Ross, Bob Rowe, Saint Jerome School, Gini Graham Scott, Susan Porrello Shimooka, Bernard Smith, Roger Smyth, Don Stevens, Chuck Strickler, James Ridgway de Szigethy, Barbara L. Tajgiszer, Bruce Thomas, (Judge) William K. Thomas, Serell Ulrich, United States Federal District Court, United States Drug Enforcement Administration, United States Marshals Service (Witness Protection Division), Ray Villani, Joe Wagner, Warrensville Heights, Ohio Police Department, Joe Wegas, Adam Wezey, Sandy Whelchel, Edward P. Whelen, Chuck Whitten, Bob Wilson, Dean Winslow, Mairy Jayn Woge, Ken Wuchte, Tom Yovich, and those persons who wished not to be named.

Special thanks to the Cleveland, Ohio Police Department, the Lyndhurst, Ohio Police Department, Frank DeMaio, Ed Kovacic, Patrick Dearden—who encouraged me to pursue this project, Heather Hall—my very capable and dedicated editor, and my Heavenly Father for His multitude of gifts, especially those of faith and perseverance.

Rick Porrello Jan. 1998

Contents

The Cleveland
La Cosa Nostra*
Circa 1980

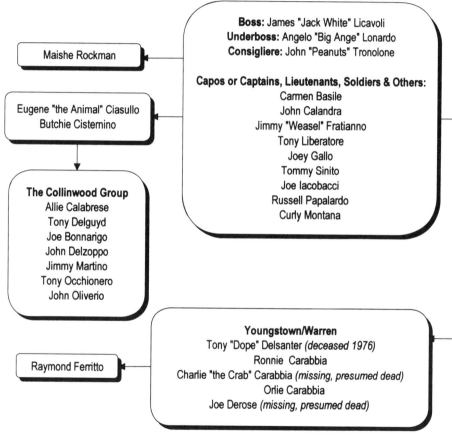

Boss: James "Jack White" Licavoli
Underboss: Angelo "Big Ange" Lonardo
Consigliere: John "Peanuts" Tronolone

Capos or Captains, Lieutenants, Soldiers & Others:
Carmen Basile
John Calandra
Jimmy "Weasel" Fratianno
Tony Liberatore
Joey Gallo
Tommy Sinito
Joe Iacobacci
Russell Papalardo
Curly Montana

Maishe Rockman

Eugene "the Animal" Ciasullo
Butchie Cisternino

The Collinwood Group
Allie Calabrese
Tony Delguyd
Joe Bonnarigo
John Delzoppo
Jimmy Martino
Tony Occhionero
John Oliverio

Youngstown/Warren
Tony "Dope" Delsanter *(deceased 1976)*
Ronnie Carabbia
Charlie "the Crab" Carabbia *(missing, presumed dead)*
Orlie Carabbia
Joe Derose *(missing, presumed dead)*

Raymond Ferritto

* The above men were alleged or reputed members, associate members or associates of the Cleveland Mafia. Sources include the Ohio Organized Crime Investigative Committee.

To Kill The Irishman - The War That Crippled the Mafia Rick Porrello 1998

The Pittsburgh La Cosa Nostra*
Circa 1984

Boss: John Sebastian LaRocca
Underboss: Joseph "Jo-Jo" Percora
Consigliere: Michael Genovese

Capos, Soldiers and Associates:
Gabriel "Kelly" Mannarino
Thomas Ciancutti
Charles Imburgia
Charles Porter
John Bazzano
Antonio Ripepi
Joseph Regino
Joseph Sica
Samuel J. Fashionatta
John C. Fontana
Michael Trafficante
Henry Zottola

Youngstown/Warren, Ohio Group

Vincent "Jimmy" Prato
Joey Naples
Lenine Strollo
Ernest Biondillo
Bernard Altshuller
Frank Lentine
Paul "Pinto" Holovatick
Peter Cascarelli

Altoona, Pennsylvania Group

Alfred Corbo
Joseph Ruggiero
John Verilla
Victor Schiappa
Carl Venturato
John Caramadre
Vincent Caraciollo
Dennis Colello

* The above men were alleged or reputed members, associate members or associates of the Pittsburgh Mafia. Sources include the Pennsylvania Crime Commission..

To Kill The Irishman - The War That Crippled the Mafia Rick Porrello 1998

The Southern California
La Cosa Nostra*
Circa 1985

Boss: Peter Milano
Underboss: Carmen Milano
Consigliere: Jack LoCicero

Capos:
Mike Rizzitello
Vincent Caci
Luigi Gelfuso Jr.

Soldiers and Associates:
Charles Caci
Stephen Cino
Rocco Zangari
Albert Nunez
Craig Fiato
Lawrence Fiato
John Demattia
John Vaccaro
Russell Masetta

* The above men were alleged or reputed members, associate members or associates of the Southern California Mafia. Sources include the California Crime Commission and the Los Angeles Times..

To Kill The Irishman - The War That Crippled the Mafia Rick Porrello 1998

The Kansas City
La Cosa Nostra*
Circa 1984

Bosses: Nick Civella
Carl "Cork" Civella
Underboss: Carl "Tuffy" Deluna
Consigliere: Unknown

Capos, Soldiers and Associates and Others:

Tony "Ripe" Civella
Peter Simone
Peter Tamburello
Charles Moretina
Tommy Lococo
Felix Ferina
Tommy Cacioppo
Willy Cammisano
Sam Ancona
Angelo Porrello

Las Vegas

Joe Agosto
Carl Thomas

* The above men were alleged or reputed members, associate members or associates of the Kansas City, Missouri Mafia. Sources include THE ENFORCER by Bill Roerner, and the FBI.

To Kill The Irishman - The War That Crippled the Mafia Rick Porrello 1998

Introduction

For decades, Americans have had a fascination with the Mafia. We have paid the box offices generously to be entertained by films like *The Godfather, Goodfellas, Casino* and *Donnie Brasco*. Likewise, millions have been spent in bookstores on titles like *Boss of Bosses, Doublecross, The Last Mafioso, Underboss* and the numerous John Gotti stories. Most recently, HBO has brought us the Sopranos.

It started in the fifties, when mob soldier Joseph Valachi broke the blood oath of *omerta* which swears Mafia members to secrecy, violations being punishable by death. The term Mafia became a household word. Higher ranking mob turncoats like Jimmy "Weasel" Fratianno, Angelo "Big Ange" Lonardo and Sammy "the Bull" Gravano would follow.

In years to come we would learn of the Mafia's influence in labor unions, gambling, political corruption, narcotics, major airports, big city docks, legitimate business and industry and even the entertainment mecca of Las Vegas. With hard-to-ignore evidence, there would be shocking allegations that the Mafia had collaborated with the Central Intelligence Agency in "Operation Mongoose," the plot to assassinate Cuban Communist leader Fidel Castro. It is even believed by many that the Mafia helped engineer the rise of John F. Kennedy to President of the United States, then was responsible for the assassinations of him, his brother Senator Robert Kennedy, and actress Marilyn Monroe.

In the seventies and eighties, the government began winning more of their battles with the Mafia. New anti-racketeering legislation and technology, coupled with tougher drug laws, undercover operations, unprecedented inter-agency cooperation and WITSEC, the federal witness protection program were effective weapons. Attrition of old-school Mafioso made the timing good. The young replacements were not the jail-stint-hardened men that their fathers, uncles and neighborhood heroes were. As a result of all this, whole Mafia hierarchies were dismantled in cities like Milwaukee, Cleveland, Kansas City and Los Angeles. Top New York mob dons, like Tony Salerno and John Gotti, were convicted and imprisoned for life.

If you trace the fall of the Italian-American Mafia to one point in time, that point would be the murder of Danny Greene. In the seventies, the fiercely proud and vicious Irishman boldly muscled in on Mafia-held rackets. He teamed up with John Nardi, an associate of Teamster bosses Bill Presser and his son, Jackie. Nardi was also the nephew of Tony Milano who was a highly-respected mob consigliere and the father of Peter Milano, Southern California La Cosa Nostra boss.

When it was apparent that the inexperienced, yet ambitious, Mafia soldiers were having no luck fulfilling their orders to kill Greene and Nardi, west coast mob capo Jimmy Fratianno stepped in. He recommended Ray Ferritto, a Pennsylvania bookmaker who proved himself when he lured the subject of a mob murder contract to a parking lot at Los Angeles International Airport, waited for a jet to take off, then shot his victim in the back of the head.

In the end, the war with Greene and Nardi would only begin to haunt La Cosa Nostra. As a result of the numerous investigations, Ferritto, Fratianno and underboss Angelo Lonardo sentenced themselves to death by betraying omerta, the Sicilian code of silence. Their testimony would help cripple Mafia families in Los Angeles, Kansas City, Milwaukee and Cleveland. Later, Fratianno would co-author his life story—*The Last Mafioso*- and he and Lonardo would help in the historic convictions of the bosses of New York's Bonnano, Colombo, Luchesse and Genovese crime families. Once the government proved that they could successfully protect Mafia informants, more mobsters became cooperating witnesses, further damaging the structure and traditions of La Cosa Nostra.

It all began with a man whom Mafia boss James Licavoli called "the Irishman"—Danny Greene.

He is descended from a race of heroes, a noble band, gold-helmed and generous. Honored, wealthy hawk of men, sturdy his limbs upon his horse; swift to accomplish overthrow in battle, a falcon excellently wise in argument, a stag who does not die. . .

*Daffy AP Gwilym—Fourteenth-century Welsh
poet on the Celtic warrior*

PART 1

Birth of the Irishman and Rise of the Mafia

Primary Characters

- Jimmy "Weasel" Fratianno: *Mafia figure*
- Danny Greene: *Longshoremens Union president and Mafia associate*
- James "Jack White" Licavoli: *Upcoming Mafia boss*
- Tony Milano: *Mafia figure*
- Leo "Lips" Moceri: *Mafia figure; cousin to Licavoli*
- John Nardi: *Vending Union official and Mafia associate*

Chapter 1

John Nardi, a 61-year-old union official, was saying good-bye to friends, business associates and relatives at the Italian-American Brotherhood Club in Little Italy. On Tuesdays, the exclusive club featured elaborate dinners attended by judges, politicians and prominent businessmen and presided over by ninety-year-old Tony Milano. During the thirties, the location served as headquarters for Tony Milano and his brother Frank, both Mafia leaders. Tony Milano, known respectfully as "the old man," was still considered consigliere, or counselor emeritus, to Cleveland's La Cosa Nostra. John Nardi, Secretary-Treasurer of Teamster Vending Machine Local 310, was a nephew by marriage to Tony Milano.

It was just past 10:00 P.M., but the area was well lit by street lights. One-hundred yards down Mayfield Road, past the popular Italian Restaurants, bakeries, bars and Holy Rosary Church, four young, nervous Mafia soldiers had concealed themselves in bushes on a railroad bridge overlooking the neighborhood. They watched the front of the Italian-American Brotherhood Club. One was aided by binoculars; another by the telescopic scope of a high-powered, semi-automatic rifle.

As John Nardi reached to unlock the door of his brand new Buick, the gunman squeezed off his first round. The sharp report sliced through the traffic noise from nearby Euclid Avenue. The would-be assassin's aim was off slightly. Nardi ducked behind the car as several more shots followed. One smashed through the driver's door. Two more shattered the windshield. Nardi was unharmed. After a few moments of wary silence, keeping his head down, he crawled through the passenger door, over the crumbled glass, put the key in the ignition and sped off.

It was September 10, 1976, and there was a vicious mob war going on in the Midwest. Nardi had recently returned from Florida, where he successfully defended himself against federal narcotics and gun-running charges. Only four months earlier, longtime Mafia boss John Scalish died during heart surgery leaving a vacuum in the local mob leadership. Nardi was a Mafia boss candidate. Tony Milano was hoping to have his son Peter return from the west coast to work with Nardi. But some local mob figures were opposed to Nardi controlling Cleveland's rackets. As a result, there were other attempts on his life.

John Nardi was a devoted family man, who enjoyed picking up his grandchildren after school and bringing them over for dinner. Those were his plans on May 17, 1977 at 3:00 P.M. after he was leaving his office. Again assassins lay in wait watching for their target to appear. But Nardi had been taking precautions. He carried a gun and had been parking in different locations. Today his car was parked near his office, in the rear of the parking lot of Teamsters Joint Council 41, across from the musicians union.

This time Nardi's stalker had his finger on a button, not a trigger. The explosion of the vehicle parked next to Nardi's rocked the area as officials and members from several labor unions ran outside helping to pull him from the fire, smoke and wreckage. Nardi's legs had been blown off.

"It didn't hurt," Nardi whispered. He was pronounced dead minutes later.

Nardi was not known as a gangster. He was a tough labor leader and a friend to many in need. The city was shocked. Cleveland had a strong labor union base, and the fatal event took place in a labor union parking lot. Many saw it as a particularly irreverent act not only against an individual, but against an institution they held dear. But Nardi was only one of many bombing victims during that dark period in Ohio's history.

Thirty-seven bombings—placing a package the gangsters called it—rocked Cuyahoga County that year, twenty-one of them in Cleveland alone, James Neff reported in his book, *Mobbed Up. The war was fought over control of illegal gambling, bookmaking, loan-sharking and labor rackets, as well as a share of the casino skim money coming from Las Vegas.*

In the end, the Mafia war resulted in unprecedented, multi-agency investigations culminating in historic convictions and treacherous mob defections from Los Angeles to Kansas City and Cleveland to New York City. Amazingly, the origins of the whole thing could be traced to one man with whom John Nardi had closely allied himself in veiled pursuit of power in the underworld. He was one unlikely man who came to be called the Irishman.

Chapter 2

On November 9, 1933, John Henry Greene and his girlfriend, Irene Cecilia Fallon appeared before a justice of the peace, and were legally married. They were both twenty-years-old and had been brought from Ireland to America as children.

Five days later Irene Greene was checked into Cleveland's Saint Ann Hospital, where all Catholic women of her time gave birth. Devastated for months by the shame and embarrassment of a child born out of wedlock, the two families were offered temporary joy in the birth of Irene's healthy baby boy.

But something went terribly wrong. Joy turned to fear. Though the delivery had gone well, the young mother developed mysterious complications. Doctors were at a loss to explain. As her condition continued to worsen, Irene Greene was moved to the intensive care ward. Several days later she died. The official cause: an enlarged heart.

It was tragedy upon tragedy which continued to take a toll on the families in years to come. The baby's identity remained simply "Baby Greene" until the tormenting funeral and burial. Afterward, John Greene decided to name his son Daniel after the baby's paternal grandfather.

Shortly after the death of his wife, John Greene began drinking heavily. He lost his job as a traveling salesman for Fuller Brush and moved in temporarily with his father, a newspaper printer, himself recently widowed. Unable and unwilling to provide for his son, Greene placed the child in an orphanage.

About ten minutes by car, south of the Cleveland city limits, is the large suburb of Parma. It was here, in 1925, on 180 acres bounded by a farm, that the world's first Catholic cottage-plan village for boys was built. A life-size statue of Jesus embracing several children still welcomes visitors. Parmadale was designed to provide homes for the rapidly growing orphan population but took in, to a larger extent, neglected and dependent children and infants, especially kids of parents who just could not afford to care for them at home. Instead, they paid a small fee for their children to be housed and educated by the nuns of Parmadale. Most of the parents, many struggling immigrants, made regular visits when their busy work schedules allowed.

The mission at Parmadale was to provide the children with a haven from fate's cruelties and turn their lives around, returning them to society with a better chance at a happy and productive life. Parmadale was successful in most cases and was hailed by professionals nation-wide. Reverend Edward Flannagan spent two weeks there before he founded his famous Boys Town.

The village started with twelve cottages set among luscious fruit orchards which proved a temptation. Periodically, some of the older boys would sneak over to a neighboring orchard and pick as much fruit as they could carry before they were discovered and chased away by the farmer. Two nuns lived with the boys in each of the cottages and tried to duplicate normal life. It was not unusual for boys to be raised to maturity at Parmadale.

In 1939, Daniel's father began dating a nurse. Within a year the couple married and moved into an apartment, soon starting their own family. Daniel, then six years old, had been recently removed from Parmadale, but ran away from his father and new stepmother several times. Once he was found hiding under a nearby porch.

Daniel was taken in by his grandfather. They lived in the upper unit of a wooden shingle, two-family house on E. 147th Street, a short block of modest single and double homes in a neighborhood known as Collinwood. Young Daniel Greene was apparently abandoned by his father. For the rest of his childhood years, he lived with his grand-father and for a time, an aunt also. When Daniel's father died in 1959, the newspaper death notice showed John Greene only as father of the children he had with his second wife. Daniel was not acknowledged.

Chapter 3

Collinwood Village sits on the south shore of Lake Erie. One of Cleveland's oldest communities, it began as a settlement of Italian and Slovenian immigrants. An expanding railway system was the basis for early development, making Collinwood one of the heaviest industrial areas in the nation. Many of the children played near the switching stations, railroad yards and tracks which divide the neighborhood roughly in half. Italians settled south of the tracks. The Waterloo area, north of the railroad, was home to Slovenians. Collinwood's White City was a waterfront park originally home to an amusement park.

Many Collinwood residents were among the 7000 workers employed at the huge Fisher Body Plant, which manufactured auto bodies. During World War II, employment swelled to 14,000 as the plant produced tank and gun parts, and engine components for B-29 planes.

Daniel Greene attended school at Saint Jerome Catholic School on Lakeshore Boulevard in Collinwood. There was no tuition for most parochial schools then, only a nominal book fee, so cost was not a factor for Daniel's grandfather.

Though bright, Daniel lacked interest in school and fit in poorly with the formal and disciplined structure of Catholic school. Separation of the sexes was strictly enforced at Saint Jerome's and most other parochial schools of the time; boys on one side of the class—girls on the other. It was the same routine at lunch, recess and mass. And at the end of the day, the students again divided in two groups—those who lived east of the school and those who lived west.

Most of the kids at Saint Jerome developed a great fondness for the nuns and priests. Even Daniel developed lasting friendships with some of his teachers, though he could often be found scowl-faced outside his classroom in the hallway where his wooden desk was moved when he misbehaved. For a time, Daniel served as an altar boy.

Daniel preferred dice games with his buddies and fights on the streets instead of school books. Often while the boys were shooting dice, the police would pull up, confiscate their change and send the boys on their way. Sometimes the cops herded the boys into the back of the cruiser and drove them around the block, letting them back off where they picked them up. The boys would be back at the same spot in a couple of days shooting dice again.

Daniel was a good friend to have. Even at a young age he was loyal and always willing to lend some change to a buddy. And he was always willing to join in a fight. Daniel was quite athletic, excelling at baseball and basketball. Even though he was a poor student who often got into trouble, the nuns of Saint Jerome let him play sports because he was too valuable to the team. He was an all-star basketball player and once won a game with seconds to go by an amazing over-head shot from mid-court.

Daniel was also on the Saint Jerome boxing team. During the forties and fifties, boxing was a popular spectator sport and many schools had teams. (Cleveland's Joey Maxim brought boxing excitement home by winning the light heavyweight championship from Freddie Mills in 1952. Maxim successfully defended the title against Sugar Ray Robinson but eventually lost it to Archie Moore.)

Daniel was an average built, handsome lad with blonde, curly hair and darting, blue eyes. Though he had little adult guidance, Daniel did have respect for his elders. Combined with his natural charm, he was well-liked by the neighborhood adults. No doubt many sympathized with this motherless boy, abandoned by his father to be raised by a grandfather who worked nights and slept days. His paper route was a lengthy task due to the mothers who would chat with him and maybe offer a bag of cookies to take home before the boy could continue on his way.

Daniel was especially liked by the McDuffy family. Sean McDuffy was in Daniel's class at Saint Jerome. But it was Billy McDuffy, eight years senior and already driving who Daniel was most fond of. He loved to run errands for Billy who was generous in compensating Daniel with whatever change he had in his pocket. Mrs. McDuffy also took a liking to the "mischievous young lad" as she called him.

Once Mrs. McDuffy gave Daniel a dollar bill to fetch her a loaf of bread from the local baker. Daniel was quick about the errand returning within ten minutes. But he caught Mrs. McDuffy's wrath bringing her two loaves of bread and the same dollar bill. Mrs. McDuffy refused to except the bread and sent Daniel back to pay for one and return the "complimentary" loaf.

Often Daniel would have friends stay over night. They usually slept on the third floor. One good friend was Joey Wagner who had run away several times going to live with Daniel. One evening the boys were out unusually late when boredom and curiosity shook hands. The boys decided to go exploring in the basement of a bar owned by future Polka king, Frankie Yankovic. Daniel kicked in the window and the boys slipped inside.

"Be quiet, they're gonna hear us," Joey cautioned.

"What are you worried about. They're all drunk up there anyhow," Daniel replied as if Joey should have known.

The two poked around carelessly in search of anything of interest. Before they were done, Daniel stole an old snare drum, bringing it home where he stored it proudly in his attic.

Daniel and Joey were in the Boy Scouts for three weeks. The boys had only joined for an excuse to get out of the house. During the first two meets, Daniel and Joey went to a local pool hall to shoot a few games. The next week they were forced to attend their first meeting since the parents had been informed that the boys would be bringing home important boy scout paperwork. It was their first and last meeting.

Daniel and Joey were late and took seats near the edge of the curtain at one end of the rough semi-circle the boys had arranged themselves in on the dusty stage. The scout master walked back and forth in front of the auditorium curtain addressing his troop. His voice echoed through the small combination gymnasium and auditorium. The scout master paused occasionally as he reviewed the honored traditions of the Boy Scouts of America. Most of the proud new scouts listened intently. Such boredom was not the evening Daniel had planned for himself.

As the scout master turned away, Daniel whispered something to Joey then quickly slipped behind the curtain. Joey's eyes widened in anticipation and fear as he glanced back and forth from the scout-master's eyes to Daniel's hand poking out from underneath the curtain. Daniel waited for the scout master to stand still, then, ever so gently managed to stick a wooden match in the space between the sole and the side of the scout master's shoe. Daniel lit the opposite end of the match tip with a lighter, then quickly slipped back around the curtain to take his seat. A few seconds later—whoosh—a "hot foot" as the tip ignited in a tiny blue and orange burst of sulfur starting the scout master into a short jig and the troop into a roar of laughter. It was a practical joke right out of a three stooges comedy, and attempted only by the most daring boys.

The scout master shouted for order while he extinguished his shoe and checked for damage. Then he conducted a very brief investigation. It wasn't difficult, since several of the boys, still snickering amongst themselves were pointing at Daniel Greene. And to further incriminate themselves, Daniel and Joey could not stop laughing.

The scout master escorted Daniel and Joey out of the school.

I'll be informing your parents of your little stunt," the scout master sternly rebuked.

Daniel certainly wasn't worried about such action.

Daniel got his first taste of the more informal and permissive life of public school at Collinwood High. He was picked up quickly by the basketball team and proved to be an excellent team player. But lack of interest in his studies was still a problem. And so were a handful of Italian ruffians. Off the basketball court Daniel was a loner, a seemingly easy target for bullying, the cocky Italians figured. But they figured wrong. Daniel feared nobody and would stand up to several boys at once, proving his talent and experience with his fists. But it was this lack of fear, this refusal to knuckle under that perpetuated bad blood between Daniel and several of the numerous Collinwood Italians in years to come.

His grandfather figured that public school was a mistake and signed Daniel up for tenth grade at Saint Ignatius Catholic High School on the west side of town. Joey Wagner also attended St. Ignatius, so he and Danny used to hitchhike to school together. One of the best hitchhiking spots had been claimed by another St. Ignatius student, a year older than Daniel and Joey. One day, Daniel decided that he wanted the spot. Despite Joey's cautions, Daniel approached the older student. He whispered something and the student turned and walked away.

"What did you say to him," Joey asked.

Daniel would only offer, "It's our spot now, Joey."

Even with his choice hitchhiking spot, Daniel found St. Ignatius High School to be a long trek. He overslept too many days and his grandfather could offer little help. He worked nights at the *Cleveland Plain Dealer* and came home too late in the morning to get the boy off to school. The routine didn't last long and Daniel was expelled. From there he went back to Collinwood High School.

But Daniel had plans of a more adventurous lifestyle which did not include school books and home work. In 1951, he dropped out of school and headed for a U.S. Marine Corps recruitment office. A few weeks later he was inducted and shipped off to Camp LeJeune, North Carolina.

Daniel served most of his time with the Marines in the Fleet Marine Force Division at Camp LeJeune where he gained respect in the boxing ring. He was transferred numerous times which may indicate that he had disciplinary problems. Still, he was promoted to corporal in 1953 and taught firearms. He was honorably discharged later that year.

Chapter 4

At the time of young Daniel Greene's birth, the nation was still suffering from the disastrous effects of October 24, 1929, the beginning of the Great Depression. In the few years following "Black Thursday," dozens of banks would fail, the unemployment rate would soar to an all-time high, homeless would flock to soup kitchens and farmers would be evicted from their land.

But in the midst of the economic plight, a sinister force was prospering, seizing the opportunity and the nation in a network that would have a tremendously negative impact on the country as it weaved its way into the very fabric of American society. The invading threads were part of a tradition bred centuries earlier across the Atlantic Ocean on the largest island in the Mediterranean. Sicily was conquered by so many different people that the natives came to distrust all forms of government. By the time Sicily became a part of the newly unified Italy, in 1861, it had seen seven governments in just one century.

Thus the Mafia was born in the 19th century. It was a secret society of honorable men who provided the poor, oppressed Sicilians with protection, stability and pride. The "vendetta" was the Sicilian form of justice. The victimized were quiet and patient. Vengeance was saved for a future time. Consequently the Mafia golden rule of "omerta" (translated as by many as "honor") was born. It became an unwritten rule to leave the government out of private affairs.

As the Mafia grew in power, its mission had been corrupted. The leaders had become greedy and hungry for power and viewed themselves as the government of the people. But for the natives, the Mafia, with all its sins, meant stability and patriotism. These traditions and attitudes were brought to America at the turn of the century as the

New World was being molded by the millions of immigrants hoping to escape poverty and oppression in the country becoming known as the Land of Opportunity.

A few immigrants, not just Sicilians and Italians but Irish, Jews, blacks and others pursued lawless enterprises in greedy searches for quick prosperity. By the twenties, most of the major cities from Chicago to New York were falling under significant influence of the underworld. Business owners threatened by bankruptcy turned to mob loansharks for cash and thus took on new partners. Powerful unions were coming under Mafia control and many high-level police officials and politicians were increasingly "on the pad."

As this force matured, battles were occurring in major cities across the nation. The struggles began with the 1919 passage of the Eighteenth Amendment and the Volstead Act forbidding the sale and manufacture of ethyl alcohol. Referred to as the "noble experiment" by President Herbert Hoover, with it came the birth of nationally organized crime. And the Mafia would become *the* organized crime force to be reckoned with.

In most cities, conflicts were being waged over booze, gambling, prostitution and their territories. In Cleveland, the most dramatic of the wars was over corn sugar, the primary ingredient of then-popular corn liquor, also known as Bourbon, a truly American whiskey, long a money crop for generations of farmers.

"Big Joe" Lonardo figured prominently in the sugar war. Around 1900, Lonardo, his three brothers, and their friends, the seven Porrello brothers, emigrated to the United States settling in Cleveland, Ohio. In 1911, Big Joe and his wife Concetta had their first son, Angelo Anthony Lonardo. His godfather was Anthony Milano, an underworld figure becoming prominent in the Little Italy district.

The Porrello and Lonardo brothers amassed small fortunes as corn sugar wholesalers. But their good fortune ended in 1927, when the Lonardo's former business manager, Salvatore "Black Sam" Todaro, engineered the murders of Joe and John Lonardo. In a five year period, ensuing bootleg violence left another Lonardo and four Porrello brothers dead.

Eighteen-year-old Angelo Lonardo swore revenge for his father's murder. He would use his unwitting mother as bait. On a sunny afternoon in 1929, Angelo drove her down to the Porrello sugar warehouse and shouted to a Porrello employee.

"Hey tell Sam Todaro that my mother wants to talk to him."

Todaro, always respectful of Big Joe's widow, approached the car unconcerned. As he got close, Angelo thrust a revolver out the window and fired six times.

When the Cuyahoga County Coroner's Office completed an autopsy on Black Sam, they noted on their report that his true name was Augusta Archangelo. After Todaro was murdered, his 8-year-old son Joseph was sent to Italy for fear that he would be killed to prevent a vendetta when he grew older. To hide his identity, the boy's last name was reportedly changed to Agosto which bore similarity to his father's real first name. Beginning in the fifties, the name Joseph Agosto began appearing in files of U.S. law enforcement agencies in the west and Midwest, exposing a mystery only partially solved in later years. During the investigation it was learned that Black Sam Todaro's son died an untimely death in Italy at the age of thirty, but his name had a new life.

Angelo Lonardo was eventually tried, convicted and sentenced to life for avenging his father's murder. But the rare success for law enforcement was short-lived. In eighteen months, clever attorneys for the Lonardo family won Angelo a second trial. Eyewitnesses responsible for the first conviction ignored subpoenas to return from Italy where they had fled in fear. Angelo was subsequently discharged and released. His successful vendetta brought him respect from Little Italy's Frank Milano to whom the former Lonardo soldiers had pledged their allegiance. In his first few years of service to the Mafia, Angelo would be instrumental in the organization of the city's black numbers operators.

Chapter 5

After the 1930 murder of Mafia boss Joe Porrello, Frank Milano and his brother Tony were the undisputed rackets powers in northeast Ohio. But it was their backing by Moe Dalitz that helped Frank Milano gain a seat on the Mafia's national ruling commission formed by New York mega-mobsters Charles "Lucky" Luciano, Meyer Lansky, Frank Costello and Nicola Gentile. It was through this notorious partnership that the transplanted concept and peoples of the Sicilian Mafia tradition was born *La Cosa Nostra* or this thing of ours—the Sicilian-American Mafia.

"All us younger guys hated the old mustaches like Maranzano and Masseria and what they was doing. We was trying to build a business that'd move with the times and they was still living a hundred years ago," Luciano explained.

The commission's crime families came to be known as the Colombos, Gambinos, Lucheses, Genoveses and the Bonannos. Frank Milano, and for a few months, Chicago's infamous Al Capone, were the only two non-New Yorkers admitted to membership during the first few decades of the commission.

In years to come, twenty-four Mafia families emerged in North America: The five New York families and one La Cosa Nostra family each in the cities of Cleveland, Los Angeles, San Francisco, Denver, Milwaukee, Chicago, Kansas City, Detroit, Saint Louis, Buffalo, Philadelphia, Boston, Providence, Pittsburgh, New Orleans, Windsor and Toronto, and in the areas of Quebec and New Jersey. In addition, numerous affiliate families would spring up in smaller towns around the primary twenty-four.

◆   ◆   ◆

It was 1888 when Tony Milano was born in the southern Italian region of Calabria. At only seven years of age he was put to work in a flour mill. At age 12 he was brought to the United States where he worked in a textile mill and on a farm in rural New York state. He was moved to Buffalo and went to work in a pool hall. After a minor brush with police in 1910, he settled in Cleveland where he founded the Italian-American Brotherhood Club in Little Italy. Colorful posters in the windows advertised upcoming Italian heritage events and picnics. In the I.A.B Club was housed Milano's Brotherhood Loan Company where Tony Milano's business was legal, profitable and simple: "no savings, just loans." Next to the club was a smaller building which came to be known as the "card shop." For decades, the card shop remained as a mob hangout and gambling room, the equivalent of one of the New York Mafia family's "social clubs."

Tony Milano also started Mayfield Importing Company with partner Al Polizzi and Tornello Importing with brother Frank, both of whom did legitimate business with their close friend from Brooklyn, New York, Joe Profaci. Much of Tony Milano's influence was in labor unions. He liked to get people jobs. He got Bill Presser the position as head of a vending machine local and the two became very close

The alliance between Jewish and Italian gangsters began in New York with Meyer Lansky and Lucky Luciano. In Cleveland, organized crime always had an Italian-Jewish partnership starting with Moe Dalitz and Frank Milano. The development of the Dalitz-Milano combination was influenced by the presence of Chuck Polizzi in Milano's Mayfield Road mob. Chuck, the adopted brother of Milano lieutenant Big Al Polizzi, was actually a Jew. The religious crossover continued in years to come with numbers kingpin Alex "Shondor" Birns who was allied with the Mafia, and finally Milton "Maishe" Rockman, brother-in-law to John Scalish.

Ralph Salerno, a former New York Police Dept. detective and organized crime expert explained once: "There is a happy marriage of convenience between Jewish and Italian gangsters. It represents the three M's: Money, Moxie and Muscle, The Jews supply the moxie. The Italians take care of the muscle. And they split the money between them."

By the 1950s, Anthony Milano was considered somewhat of a patriarch in Little Italy. He was known respectfully as "Mister Tony" or "The Old Man." But it had not always been that way. He claimed that discrimination caused bloodshed in Little Italy in the early part of the century.

"The other Italians did not want the Sicilians or Calabrians here," Milano told a reporter once. "They would not give us housing because of the Mafioso reputation. I straightened that up," he once boasted.

The Milanos and Moe Dalitz became interested in gambling when the end of rumrunning seemed inevitable. The mighty combine began opening, or muscling control of casinos in and around northeast Ohio. Some of the better known ones included the Thomas Club, the Harvard Club, the Arrowhead, the Pettibone Club and the Mounds Club.

The Ohio Villa, in suburban Richmond Heights Village was Milano's property and first site of the Tuesday night nine-course dinners that later made the Italian-American Brotherhood Club famous. Perry Como was a favored performer at the Villa where Italian heritage picnics and events were held. The Ohio Villa was renamed the Richmond Country Club. It eventually burned.

In the late thirties, the Dalitz-Milano combination started looking south toward the Ohio River area for promising gambling turf. Law Enforcement in Cleveland was getting tough with the arrival of Eliot Ness who, as Safety Director, cleaned up much police corruption. Conversely, the Kentucky and Ohio border region was known for its lax enforcement of the law. During Prohibition, disputes were settled with a six-shooter and the area became known as "Little Mexico." The Cleveland gangsters took over the Coney Island Race Track outside of Cincinnati and renamed it River Downs. They operated huge gambling operations like the Continental Supper Club in Chesapeake, Ohio.

In Newport, Kentucky, profits from the Lookout House Casino were shared with newcomer James Licavoli from St. Louis. Gambling in Newport operated without interference for two decades due to mob-installed county officials. Best known of the gaming houses was the plush Beverly Hills Supper Club in Covington, Kentucky. Opened in 1937, the Beverly Hills was billed as the "Showplace of the nation" and "America's finest and most beautiful supper club." Constructed at a cost of $300,000, the Beverly Hills Club was an impressive colonial building housing several rooms including a large cocktail bar room and a main stage that featured top Broadway and Hollywood entertainment. Eight huge mirrors lined the entrance way to the silver and coral-blue painted foyer. And of course, a plush casino at the Beverly Hills offered slot machines, crap tables, blackjack, bingo, roulette and chuck-a-luck. Gross annual earnings in 1940 were said to be over $500,000.

Chapter 6

Many Little Italy teenagers hung around the Mayfield Road Italian-American Brotherhood Club, idolizing the tough wiseguys, their flamboyant, mysterious lifestyles, fancy cars and clothing. In a back room at the I.A.B. Club, the Milano henchmen played Pinochle or Ziganetta while their bosses held court.

Among the many who fell in with the gangsters were Jimmy "Weasel" Fratianno and John Nardi. Fratianno's nickname had come from earlier years while the boy was being chased by police after stealing some fruit.

"Look at that little weasel run," one cop remarked.

Born Aladena Fratianno in Naples, Italy, in 1913, Jimmy was brought to the United States as a young boy and settled in Cleveland. He developed a knack for making money in the rackets—an "earner" in mob talk. When Jimmy was old enough to drive, he became a driver for an associate of Moe Dalitz. He chauffeured gamblers to the different clubs for seven dollars a load. Jimmy was making more money booking at local racetracks, so the enterprising young racketeer bought a used Marmon limousine and hired a driver to keep his chauffering business going. In months to come Jimmy and his friend Louis "Babe" Triscaro were drafted as baseball bat-swinging, picket line soldiers for the struggling Teamsters Union. Shortly afterward, Fratianno was convicted of robbery and spent eight years in prison before heading west.

John Nardi was born Giovanni Narcchione in Cleveland, in 1916. He earned his first police record entry in 1939, at the age of 23. He had been employed by a vending workers union to sell the services of their repair technicians. Sometimes he was too enthusiastic. When Nardi threatened a bar owner with serious physical harm, Safety

Director Eliot Ness ordered him arrested. Eventually the charges were dropped, but the experience proved valuable since Nardi would later represent the interests of his uncle Tony Milano with Ohio Teamster leader and jukebox baron Bill Presser.

By the late forties, Nardi had been taken on by Presser as a partner in several jukebox companies. During that time, Nardi was also running a Little Italy booking operation with Jimmy Fratianno. Not long after Nardi married into the Milano family, Tony Milano got him into Teamsters Vending Machine Service Employees Local 410, which was founded by Bill Presser. In later years, John Nardi was elected Secretary-Treasurer.

As younger men, hanging around the Italian-American Brotherhood Club, Nardi and Fratianno met other important gangsters like Johnny Scalish and little Frankie Brancato. Scalish was a burglar and robber for the Mayfield Road Mob. Senior mob members considered him a "stand up" guy, a quiet, efficient and trustworthy worker with a good future. Later Scalish was drafted as a clerk at the Pettibone Club and in Room 504 of the Garfield Hotel, yet another Syndicate gambling spot.

Frankie Brancato got his start in the underworld after working as a longshoreman on the New York City docks. Those were the same docks that fell under the control of the Gambino crime family in the sixties. Though diminutive in size, Brancato was a feared independent gunman suspected in the 1932 murders of corn sugar dealers Raymond and Rosario Porrello. Several hours after they were gunned down, a man made his way into a west side emergency room.

"I have a pain in my stomach," he complained to the attending doctor.

Examination revealed a gunshot wound hastily dressed with gauze. The man's name: Frank Brancato.

"I was shot in a fight on the west side," Brancato insisted when questioned by police.

After a successful innovative surgical procedure performed by Dr. Joseph Romano, police took the slug to their ballistics expert. They figured right. The bullet came from one of the same guns used in the Porrello murders. Brancato refused to change his story. He was charged and convicted of perjury, and sent to prison for several years.

Two years later, Frank Milano sailed to Vera Cruz, Mexico, leaving behind an indictment for income tax evasion. Milano would spend winters on his Columbia Plantation in Jesus Carranza where he maintained interests in coffee, lumber and oil. He was well liked by the Mexican Indians for his concern of their welfare and even became knowledgeable in several of their dialects. He was also identified as a major player in the illegal importation of Mexican farm workers.

Officially, Milano left his lieutenant Big Al Polizzi in charge. Polizzi was a veteran of the newspaper circulation and sugar wars. Unofficially it was still Moe Dalitz though who had the bigger connections, particularly with powerful mobsters. Tony Milano split his time between Los Angeles and Cleveland where he continued to wield much power from his Little Italy base. He had luxurious homes on Sunset Boulevard in Beverly Hills, Watseka Avenue in Palms, California and Beverly View Drive in Los Angeles.

On the west coast, Tony and Frank Milano along with Jack Dragna, Johnny Roselli and Nick Licata ranked high in Southern California Mafia. Organized crime there had a late start, never developing as much power as the mob outfits in the east and Midwest. The F.B.I. would keep tabs on men like the Milanos as part of the "Top Hoodlum Program." An F.B.I. report from 1952 revealed just how influential Tony Milano was. The information was gleaned from a confidential informant.

[Informant] advised that TONY "OLD MAN" MILANO is the head man in the Los Angeles Mafia. . . Informant stated MILANO may be residing in Cleveland, Ohio or Los Angeles, California, but he maintains control of the "Italian group" in Los Angeles. The informant stated that in comparison to MILANO, JACK DRAGNA could be considered just a puppet, and MILANO'S power over Italians in Los Angeles resembles that of a king and his word is law to his followers. Informant advised MILANO maintained a residence on Sunset Boulevard (9451 Sunset Boulevard, Beverly Hills, California), and while residing in Los Angeles has some 50 or 60 henchman at his beck and call whom he can call together at a moment's notice in order to carry out any requests. . . Informant advised that in *his opinion MILANO was probably the most powerful man in the United States insofar as the criminal element among Italians is concerned. Informant stated, however, that in spite of this power, MILANO has avoided publicity, keeps in the background, and as a consequence is not as widely known as some of the other key figures.*

Eventually Tony Milano returned to Cleveland, leaving behind sons Peter and Carmen, who would eventually takeover leadership of Southern California's La Cosa Nostra in the seventies.

Chapter 7

In the early forties, Jimmy Fratianno met James Licavoli, whose real name was Vincentio "James" Licavoli. In St. Louis, James Licavoli and his cousins, Peter and Thomas, better known as "Yonnie," were bootleggers.

James Licavoli was born in Sicily, the third of four children born of Dominic and Girolama Licavoli. They emigrated to the United States and eventually settled in St Louis with other members of their family.

In 1926, James was shot in the leg and arrested after a wild chase and shootout with St Louis police. Though he had fired on police, James was charged merely with carrying a concealed weapon and even that charge was dropped. Later, James followed his cousins to Detroit where they had wrested control of the city's racket's from the original Purple Gang. There a bootleg conviction cost him a stint at Leavenworth. When he was released he joined his cousins in Toledo, Ohio, where they moved to avoid heat from the murder of a crusading Anti-Mafia radio broadcaster, Jerry Buckley.

The Licavolis and their cousin, Leo Moceri, were not in Ohio long. Yonnie and four others of his gang were arrested for the murder of a Toledo beer baron. Pete Licavoli returned to Detroit and regrouped - his force retaining the Purple Gang title. James Licavoli hid in Pittsburgh where he stayed with up-and-coming mob boss John Sebastian LaRocca. Later he returned to Cleveland and became close friends with Jimmy Fratianno and Tony "Dope" Delsanter. Among their exploits at the time, they teamed up to rob northeast Ohio gambling halls. Licavoli was "made" into the Cleveland family two years later. He became wealthy from vending machines and gambling enterprises.

During the early forties, the Cleveland Syndicate's immensely profitable gambling casinos were shut down, one after another, by the police. Dalitz and his boys were hungry for other less risky, more respectable, money-making opportunities. An investment opportunity being sought by Cleveland nightclub owner Norman Khoury, sparked their interest. Khoury was excited by a stretch of Nevada desert slowly coming to life as Las Vegas, but his deal had fallen through.

The timing was good for Dalitz but bad for New York mobster Bugsy Siegel who had accurately envisioned Las Vegas as an immensely profitable gambling and entertainment center. Siegel had fallen out of the good graces of his fellow gangland brethren due to his reckless handling of their investment money. He was shot numerous times in the head by a sniper concealed outside his Beverly Hills mansion .

Siegel's plush Flamingo Hotel and Casino, the first of its kind on the fledgling Las Vegas Boulevard "Strip" needed competent leadership if its mob financiers were to avoid a major loss. The New York mob chose Moe Dalitz to head out to Nevada and look things over. Dalitz was intelligent and had a clean record. He would make a good a "strawman," or front man, with no criminal history to raise the suspicions of law enforcement officials.

In the meantime, a San Diego nightclub owner, named Wilbur Clark, had poured capital into Las Vegas by beginning construction of the Desert Inn Hotel and Casino. Clark had fallen short of the funds he needed to complete construction, so Dalitz and the Cleveland Syndicate stepped in to "help." They supplied the rest of the money to Clark who became their strawman.

Anticipating major profits from the Desert Inn, Dalitz bought an insurance policy. He gave his Mayfield Road partners in Cleveland, namely the Milano brothers, Al Polizzi and John Scalish a share in the Desert Inn to prevent another Mafia family from muscling in later. It was this style of thinking that would raise Dalitz to the top corridors of power in both the underworld and overworld.

Chapter 8

By the late forties, Jimmy "Weasel" Fratianno and Leo "Lips" Moceri had settled in California. Moceri acquired his nickname because of his thick lips. At age thirty-three, Fratianno became a made member of the west coast Mafia family headed by Jack Dragna.

Moceri and Fratianno had proven themselves as cold-blooded killers and often reminisced about some of their hits while playing Pinochle. On one occasion Leo told Jimmy about the decade-old murder of Les Brunemann at a restaurant in Redondo Beach, California. The hit was ordered by Los Angeles Mafia boss Jack Dragna after Brunemann threatened Johnny Roselli, a Chicago mobster stationed out west. After a failed attempt by an L.A. mob soldier, Moceri was given the contract.

"Now listen to this Jimmy," Moceri recalled. "I've got a forty-five automatic and the place's packed with people. I walk right up to his table and start pumping lead. Believe me, that sonovabitch's going to be dead for sure this time. . ."

In the years to follow, Fratianno and Moceri split up but remained close friends. Jimmy also stayed close to several Cleveland and Youngstown mobsters and made frequent trips to Ohio. Leo eventually moved to Akron, Ohio, fifty miles south of Cleveland, where he kept busy with his cousin Jack Licavoli who was making a mint from the infamous Jungle Inn. Assisting Licavoli was Tony Delsanter. Frank Brancato also had a piece of the action.

Originally a brothel, the Jungle Inn was an open casino offering huge crowds of gamblers craps, barbut, chuck-a-luck, roulette, cards and even Bingo for the ladies. It was operated by Mike Farah for Jack Licavoli. Over its years of existence, numerous murders and disappearances were traced to the casino and its operators and associates.

Jim Mancini alias "Muncene" was gunned down in 1941 after trying to monopolize control of nearby dog tracks. His convicted killer was a hired gun associated with Jack Licavoli. Licavoli was also a suspect in the murder of slot machine czar Nate Weisenberg. He was blown away in 1945 by a horrific shotgun blast to the face. Licavoli hid out in Youngstown where he lived for several weeks in a downtown hotel. He was finally arrested but was released for insufficient evidence. It was said Weisenberg was murdered for failing to deal acceptably with Youngstown and Cleveland mobsters. Even Jungle Inn manager Mike Farah fell victim to gang guns. He started giving Jack Licavoli problems and was reportedly killed by Tony Delsanter.

Through the intervention of Governor Frank J. Lausche in 1949, local, state and federal officials succeeded in closing down the Jungle Inn.

PART 2
The Rise of Danny Greene

Primary Characters

♦ Shondor Birns: *Gambling racketeer and Mafia associate*

♦ Frank Brancato: *High-ranking Mafia figure*

♦ Pete DiGravio: *Operator of lucrative loan business*

♦ Mike Frato: *Rubbish Hauler; friend of Greene*

♦ Danny Greene: *Union Official; Mafia associate*

♦ Ed Kovacic: *Police Officer*

♦ Sam Marshall: *Newspaper reporter*

♦ Art Snepeger: *Danny Greene henchman*

Chapter 9

After being honorably discharged from the Marines in 1952, Daniel Greene moved to New York City where he met New Yorker June Tears. The couple fell in love, moved to Cleveland and were married. Danny took a job as a brakeman in the Collinwood rail yards.

The marriage didn't last long and brought no children. In 1954, Daniel left his wife and filed for divorce alleging "gross neglect of duty and extreme cruelty" by June Thomas Tears Greene. The court issued its decision in 1956:

> . . .The court further finds that as alleged in the petition the defendant had a husband living at the time of marriage from which the divorce is sought and that by reason thereof plaintiff is entitled to the relief prayed for. (Divorce granted Feb. 29th, 1956)

How devastating—a bigamous bride! Greene apparently recovered quickly. In 1955, he met an attractive brunette named Nancy. He told her nothing of his marriage to June Tears and before that divorce was granted, Daniel and Nancy married. They stayed together five years and had two daughters. In 1960, Nancy filed for divorce accusing Daniel of gross neglect of duty.

In the meantime, Daniel's tangled romantic history continued. In 1961 he married again, and fathered two sons and another daughter. Shortly after, Daniel left the railroads and went to work on the docks as a stevedore. He became a popular member of Local 1317 of the

International Association of Longshoremen. It was about this time that the country got its first big break in the fledgling war on organized crime. Joseph Valachi, a soldier in New York's Genovese crime family had been sentenced to death by Vito Genovese. It was under this pressure that he agreed to cooperate with the federal government.

"For the first time, an insider—a knowledgeable member of the racketeering hierarchy—has broken the underworld's code of silence," Attorney General Robert Kennedy commented of Valachi. "Valachi's disclosures are more important for another reason. In working a jigsaw puzzle, each piece tells us something about the whole picture and enables us to see additional relationships. It is the same in the fight against organized crime. Valachi's information [adds] essential detail and brings the picture into sharper focus. . . The picture is an ugly one. It shows what has aptly been described as a private government of organized crime, a government with an annual income of billions, resting on a base of human suffering and moral corrosion."

◆　　◆　　◆

The sixties were the glory years for the Cleveland Port. The growth began with the 1959 opening of the Saint Lawrence Seaway which added 8,300 miles of sea coast to the United States and Canada. With access to the Atlantic Ocean, immensely profitable overseas trade was made possible for 95,000 square miles of freshwater lakes in the states of Ohio, Minnesota, Wisconsin, Michigan, Illinois, Indiana, Pennsylvania and New York, and the Canadian provinces of Ontario and Quebec.

Cleveland spent $10 million to ready the waterfront for the arrival of overseas shipping. At its peak, the northern Ohio port city averaged nine thousand ships through the harbor, dropping off twenty-one million tons of iron ore, automobiles, grain and general merchandise annually; a figure that had tripled in ten years. They were impressive numbers for a relatively small port that was ice-locked four months out of the year.

Unloading ships is tough, hectic and dangerous work. It is second only to mining in work-related injuries and deaths. A prayer was even composed in the early sixties after two longshoremen were killed in work-related accidents. The "Stevedore's Prayer" was believed to be the first written specifically for longshoremen. It received the approval of the Catholic Church and was introduced at a special open-air mass on the waterfront. The prayer read as follows:

Lord Your name is holy, help us to remember it.
You worked beside the lake like we do;
Your eye is our signalman;
Your pallet of grace holds every load;
Your strength lightens every lift;
These works are our daily bread.
Forgive us when overtime in work or sin
makes us undermine you.
Help us to forgive our enemies.
Our labor is Your labor.
Every day we handle Your cargo.
Watch over us, Lord, body and soul,
You know how much we need You.
One of these days we will come Your way.
Amen.

Not every injury or death was an accident. In 1960, stevedore official Sigvald Refsnes caught Danny Greene sleeping on-duty in the hold of a ship, and fired him. A few days later, a heavy piece of machinery fell on Refsnes, seriously injuring his leg. Refsnes spent several months recuperating, but eventually had to have his leg amputated. He could never prove any wrongdoing on the part of Greene or his longshoremen buddies, but the timing was suspicious, to say the least.

Longshoremen work in gangs. There are greenhorns who drop into the holds of the ship to strap and chain giant containers of cargo. Signalmen give heavy crane operators the okay to raise the load up. Cowhides were worst for the men in the hold because maggots and salt would fall on them as the loads were being raised. The favored workers might get a gravy assignment like checking. They merely wait for the pallets to be extracted from the ship and then inventory the load with a tally sheet. Other dock workers used lift trucks to warehouse the cargo.

Longshoring is a small but furious world of winches, crates, pallets, lifts, cranes and diesel smoke. If a ship ports during the night, the longshoremen might have to work in foggy, damp weather. Often workers are transients with questionable backgrounds. But still there is a strong camaraderie among these often foul-mouthed, tough-talking, bluest of blue-collar workers. Bill Sammon, writing for the Cleveland Plain Dealer, observes the beginning of a day on the docks.

> . . . *In a clapboard shack at the bottom of a hill, . . . a ragtag group of men gather on the waterfront. Their aging cars and rusting pickups putter past Dock 32 in the first hours of sunlight. Skylark, Thunderbird, Mustang, Cutlass Supreme. Not a foreign set of wheels in the bunch. Lake Erie laps languidly against the wharf as the men, bull-necked and barrel-chested, rub sleep from their eyes. Weather-beaten paws nurse coffees and smokes. . .*
>
> *"Hey," one man calls out cheerily to a friend. "What the (expletive) you doin'?"*
> *"Nothin'. It's (expletive) cool today."*
> *"Yeah. And there's (expletive) boats all over the place!"*
>
> *And so begins another day of tirelessly conjugating the all-purpose curse word. It is an epithet much favored by the salty, rough and tumble pugs known as longshoremen.*

The shack Sammon refers to was the local 1317 hiring hall, a shanty next to the union hall where the men who wanted to work that day would gather in the morning. It is called a "shape up"—a crude, casual method of employment selection once abolished at some ports. To get work, men called a special phone line at union headquarters. A tape recording, updated daily, gave the dock number, the number of gangs needed and starting times. Those who wanted to work that day would meet for the shape-up, each with the hope of being chosen to receive a work ticket entitling them to a day's wages.

Daniel Greene became popular with the other longshoremen or "dockwallopers" as they have also been dubbed on the Great Lakes.

He had quite a charismatic personality and developed friends and followers easily. But Daniel apparently decided that his future was not going to be one of such manual labor.

In his spare time Greene busied himself reading. One of his favorites was Leon Uris' *Trinity*, a true-to-life novel about Irish oppression by the British. He also read *On The Waterfront* about corruption on the docks of New York City. Daniel was especially fond of books about Celtic and Irish history, particularly the legends of the fearless Celtic warriors. It was a part of his past he could be proud of.

The Celts were one of the great barbarian peoples of Europe during the 500 years before birth of Christ. They were known for their ferocious and skilled warriors and were a people almost constantly at war pursuing conquests and new land but eventually being conquered by the Roman Empire.

Most of the Celtic men were tall, fair, and blonde or redheaded with mustaches. They were unusually clean for their era and were well built, being very conscious of their physiques even to the point that obesity-prone warriors were fined. They were an impetuous people with extravagant pride. Some tribes undressed completely before going into battle, showing off their impressive builds and heavy gold jewelry while taunting their enemies. The Celtic warriors cultivated two arts with great success: the art of clever speech, and the art of war.

The Celts believed that after death, they joined the very gods they worshipped. For them, death was the center of a long life, not the end. Celtic warriors were not afraid of death. They would consider it an insult to their honor to run from a collapsing building. Certainly this lack of fear fed their courage. Above all else, the Celtic warrior wanted to be remembered as a hero whose exploits would live on in history.

This was the history of the Celts. But in time, it seems that this was also the mindset of Daniel Greene. It was also the mindset and spirit of Danny Greene. In time, it would be obvious that Danny was emulating the brave warriors of his ancestry. Perhaps it was, at least in part, the reading about his noble roots that fueled a hidden ambition.

Chapter 10

In 1961, Walter Weaver, president of Local 1317 of the International Longshoremen's Association, ran into some hot water for operating as an employer in contracts for the unloading of grain ships. Unions were created to unite workers for the improvement of their working conditions and fringe benefits. To operate as an employer was an obvious conflict of interest. When Weaver was removed from office, the international president met with the union officers in search of someone to run things until an election could be arranged to choose a new local president. Apparently he was most impressed with Greene because he appointed him as trustee to run the local in the interim. When the election was held, Greene won the vote.

A new Daniel Greene was born. He had real power at last as the president of Local 1317 of the International Longshoremen's Association. He began introducing himself as Danny. Greene was also elected as district vice president of the Great Lakes Office of the I.L.A. The I.L.A. was organized on the Great Lakes around 1895. By 1925 the union had gained influence in nearly every U.S. port. During this period, Irish immigrants controlled most major ports except for New York where the Italians were the dominating group.

On his lapel, Danny wore a custom-designed diamond-studded I.L.A. pin. His hair had darkened a bit since his days as a blonde child and was more wavy than curly. He had a ruggedly handsome face with some pock-marking and full lips. His naturally high forehead was accentuated by hair loss which he eventually minimized with painful transplants.

To start, Danny ordered the I.L.A. headquarters cleaned up and kept that way. Even the bathroom sparkled and seldom could a piece of litter be found in the union hall parking lot. Like the Celtic warriors,

Greene took his personal hygiene very seriously. He even had a nail brush in the union bathroom to keep his well-manicured nails scrubbed clean.

Danny had a section of the union building remodeled into a proud and spacious office for himself. It was outfitted with plush, green carpeting and rich mahogany furniture. Centered on his impressive desk was a stiletto stuck into a block of cork. A meeting room was furnished with a huge mahogany table. In later months, Danny would begin hosting parties at the I.L.A. hall before and after Cleveland Browns games. Among his guests were judges and councilmen.

"Before I got here, union headquarters was a closet with a packing crate and a light bulb on a cord," Greene laughed.

The sprucing up of the union hall included a fresh coat of paint. The color? Green. It would go well with Danny's new green Cadillac and green-ink pens. He purchased baseball-style ILA jackets (green with white leather sleeves) for his handful of officers and loyalists whom he dubbed his "Inner Circle." The color green was an obsession that became Danny's trademark. He even had the union by-laws reprinted in green ink and used green paper to post announcements on the union bulletin board.

Danny was equally impassioned in his liking of Democrats. Paintings of former Presidents Harry S. Truman and Franklin D. Roosevelt hung on his office walls. In his bookshelf were *The Last Hurrah*, about the life of James Michael Curley, former Boston mayor, and *The Enemy Within*, by former U.S. Attorney Robert Kennedy. Near his desk were bronzed busts of the late President John F. Kennedy and Jacqueline Kennedy. Proudly displayed between them was a mint, Kennedy half dollar in a presentation case.

Most of Greene's initial changes drew little more than chatter from the I.L.A. members, but some caused quite a stir. For instance, he ordered the lobby window closed and locked thus eliminating the open view of the inside offices that members and visitors previously had. Instead he had a single, in-house phone placed in the lobby. Members and visitors would have to pick up the phone and explain their presence in this forbidding place to someone on the other side. Then, maybe, they would be seen by one of Danny's officers or under rare circumstances Danny himself. For members coming in simply to pay dues, they just had to drop their money in a dues slot newly built into the locked office door.

Danny kept a newly-purchased pistol in his desk drawer. Like the Celtic warriors who constantly honed their battle skills, Greene practiced target-shooting in the union hall at night. To provide security for the hall and to run errands, Danny hired ex-boxer and railroad buddy Arthur Snepeger.

During his first and one of very few meetings with the membership, Danny raised the annual dues by about 25%. He also fired more than fifty members.

"They were all winos and drifters," he declared to the other members.

Some of the members complained about the changes, which distanced them from their labor representatives and made a fortress out of their union hall. Danny seemed to have a mysterious perception about who was saying what, who was complaining, and who might be provoking others. Rumors caused fear among the workers that some of them were spying for Greene. It was a mystery to be solved in months to come.

As a new union official, Danny frequented the night spots on downtown's Short Vincent Avenue, named for its diminutive length. Though tiny in size, Short Vincent was the festive hub of Cleveland's entertainment district in the sixties. In the middle of the little block, was the venerable Theatrical Bar and Grille where bookies and B-girls rubbed elbows with well-to-do tourists, suburbanites, attorneys and judges. A few doors down, the exotic dancers from the Roxy Theater displayed their wares for the younger, male crowd. Big Ange Lonardo operated the Tastee Barbecue and later the Frolics Bar on Short Vincent before he became a partner in Captain Frank's Seafood Restaurant on the East Ninth Street pier. Few knew of his mob background at the time. He was known as a successful restaurateur.

The Theatrical was founded and run by newspaper circulation war and racing wire service veteran Morris "Mushy" Wexler. For decades, it was the social headquarters for many Clevelanders, including organized crime figures. Featuring fine food and top entertainers on its elevated stage in the center of a circular bar, the Theatrical was a favorite stop for visiting celebrities.

Veteran Cleveland reporter Doris O'Donnell wrote: Eddie Duchin headed for the Theatrical between shows at the Palace Theater. It was at the Theatrical that Edward G. Robinson dined after playing the Hanna Theater, where Toots Shor satisfied his professional interest in foods when in Cleveland. Lauren Bacall's nightly visits via limousine with an entire Hanna Theater cast were the talk of the town. . . Regulars at the Theatrical when their gigs brought them to town included Frank Sinatra, George Jessel, Milton Berle, Victor Borge, Jimmy Durante. . . and they listened to such piano stylists as Ellie Frankel.

It was at the Theatrical where Danny Greene took a liking to a waitress there and hired her as a union secretary. He provided her with a new car, raffling off an old one to the members—a seemingly generous move. The members were all issued raffle tickets, even those not interested in the car. A letter from Greene accompanied the tickets. It read in part:

You have been issued five (5) books of tickets for which you are responsible, regardless of whether you sell them or lose them. The face value of the tickets is $30.00.

At the Theatrical, Danny met Shondor Birns and Frank Brancato. Birns, enjoying his golden years, was still active in the numbers racket, enforcing peace among the mostly black operators. Brancato had something in common with Greene—he had also been a longshoreman in his younger days. Now "Frank B." was an honored partner in the small but mighty Licatese faction of the Cleveland Mafia, headed by John DeMarco and aligned with the larger and better known Scalish regime.

DeMarco and Scalish had been laying low after receiving extra media attention from their arrests at the 1957 raid on the national Mafia gathering in Apalachin, New York. There, dozens of top mobsters attended a failed crime convention which recalled memories of the 1928 gathering in Cleveland. The guest lists included Joe Bonanno, Vito Genovese and Joe Profaci from New York, Sam Giancana from

Chicago, Frank DeSimone from Los Angeles and John LaRocca and Mike Genovese from Pittsburgh.

A reporter approached Scalish for a comment about his attendance at the mob gathering.

"You can blabber all you want," Scalish said. "I can't stop you."

One of Danny Greene's West Side social spots was the Blue Fox Restaurant and Lounge. There Danny could often be found with Adrian "Junior" Short. Since 1965, Short had been president of local 27 of the International Association of Theatrical Stage Employees. He ruled the stagehands local like a personal fiefdom using the hiring hall and intimidation. He was said to carry a .22 in his jacket and keep a sawed-off shotgun in his desk drawer.

Birns, Brancato, Short and Louis "Babe" Triscaro took a liking to Greene. He was young, tough, ambitious and bold and they enjoyed his company. Perhaps he brought back memories of their glory days. Triscaro was a former champion boxer who started into the labor movement as a business agent for the truckers' union. From there he worked his way up to President of Teamsters Local 436.

As Vice President of Teamster Joint Council 41, Triscaro became close friends with Detroit labor leader, James Riddle Hoffa, the youngest man to be elected to the national executive board of the Teamsters. Triscaro was a major supporter of Hoffa, helping him win the presidency of the International Brotherhood of the Teamsters in the sixties.

Though Babe Triscaro found himself targeted by the F.B.I. Top Hoodlum program, he was greatly admired by workers in northeast Ohio where he made generous contributions to the community. He was instrumental in the organization of many laborers groups including electrical suppliers, plumbers, glass and lumber workers. Triscaro was also praised justly by the public sector for his charitable work. He arranged important donations, including providing the nation's first wheel-chair iron lung to a Cleveland hospital.

Danny set up a side business with Triscaro who had a day laborer service. When extra hands were needed on the docks, Greene hired them from Triscaro's labor service. To maintain eligibility to work, the employee had to pay a work fee.

hapter

Danny's tenure at the I.L.A. was marked by controversy after controversy. He was a tough and often stubborn negotiator. He didn't care what the price was, he just wanted his way. On the surface, it often appeared that Danny really had the welfare of his union members in mind.

For instance, he insisted on having I.L.A. line men, the men who tie the ship up when it docks, work the incoming vessels. But when one shipping company insisted on using its own anchor men, Danny just sent in the least experienced and slowest I.L.A. linemen. Some of the rank and file members also adopted this hostile attitude toward the stevedore companies. Greene's inner circle created nightly havoc with shootings, small bombings and beatings of dissident longshoremen.

When the shipping companies threatened to start docking sixty miles to the east in Ashtabula, Ohio, Danny shut down the Cleveland port and forced their hand. Finally, stevedore officials were forced to sit down with the brazen Danny Greene.

"The union will hold the hiring hall in one central place. Tell us how many gangs you need and we will choose the men.," Greene demanded. "In addition, I'll stop all this strife that is costing you daily."

The stevedore officials had no choice and were losing thousands of dollars everyday. With no leverage to negotiate, they signed a collective bargaining agreement which gave the I.L.A., i.e. Greene, the exclusive privilege to pick and employ workers on the docks. The stevedore companies paid an average of $4,000 to Greene for the unloading of each ship and he supplied the manpower.

"The hiring hall is a place where Irish kids can get a decent day's wages," Danny explained to the longshoremen about the change.

In reality, it was a significant part of Greene's calculated plan to obtain dictatorial power on the docks. He could now give the best jobs to his most loyal henchmen. Those who complained simply starved.

It was about this time that Danny received a phone call from an F.B.I. agent investigating a longshoreman. The dock worker, one of Greene's inner circle, had left a gun in his Detroit hotel room after attending an I.L.A. convention. The agent, Marty McCann, made an appointment to speak with Danny about the incident. McCann headed up a newly established organized crime squad and was well known for his ability to develop informants. Though courageous and determined, McCann was also personable and approachable—many of Greene's own traits. And of course, McCann was of Irish descent. It was no wonder that Greene and McCann hit it off.

Once the hiring hall agreement was in effect, Danny negotiated another contract with Sherwin-Williams and International Milling to pay the I.L.A. a lump sum for the unloading of their grain and flax, used to make paints, flour and cereal. The union then issued paychecks to the longshoremen.

From these grain loads, Danny pressed for "voluntary" paycheck deductions to go toward a newly-established building fund to be used for remodeling the union hall. Some of the longshoremen were told they could donate $25.00 in cash to the fund, but most opted to volunteer their time unloading the grain boats.

Like cowhides, grain is among the most dreaded loads for longshoremen. The work is dusty, hot and dangerous. Fortunately, about two-thirds of the grain is unloaded via an enclosed conveyor that is sent into the hold pulling the product out and transferring it directly into the storage building. But then the crews must take over donning protective masks to prevent their lungs from filling with dust. They descend into the grain hold and wade around in up to fifteen feet of grain or flax seed, then guide mechanical plows to scoop the leftover grain onto the conveyor.

A longshoreman unloading grain worked only one half hour in these nasty conditions. He emerged from the hold soaked with sweat and covered with dust. In the winter, he ran to a buddy's car to keep warm for his half hour break. At the end of payday, the men endorsed their checks and turned them over to union officials. But it didn't stop there. For many, what was supposed to be six or ten hours of donated time, turned into 100, 200 even 300 hours of free work. Those who complained or refused to work the grain boats were all but forced into retirement on the docks. For most, this was not an option because they knew no other way to make a living. If they were picked for any work during the morning shape-up, it was for the filthiest, toughest jobs. Skilled machine operators might even wind up in the ship's hold unloading maggot-infested cowhides.

Most went along with the scam to continue their eligibility for other work. Some left the docks to pursue different employment. A few of the most persistent members were kept in line, tough-talked or strong-armed by the few union bosses and timekeepers in the gang that did get paid. It was shake-down city at the Cleveland International Longshoremen's Association and Danny Greene was making money—and a reputation.

But longshoremen are a tough lot. They began complaining to vice president Chauncey Baker. Originally one of Greene's inner circle, Baker became a popular and influential officer who had recruited many of the dock workers. The complaints turned to heated allegations and Baker then approached Greene.

"Danny, we've got to stop the grain ship volunteering," he warned.

The operation was putting too much money in Danny's pocket. By that time, he had moved Nancy and their two daughters to a stately home in the Cleveland suburb of Willoughby. For protection, he bought a German Shepherd dog. Danny's greed clouded his judgement, and he rejected the well-meant advice.

"No, We continue. And you know what Chauncey? Maybe we should part. I'm putting you back on the docks."

Seeing Baker as a threat to his control, Greene assigned him to a small area of the dock hoping to reduce his influence among the longshoremen. Then he called in Chauncey's brother, John, an I.L.A. business agent.

"Where do you stand in this argument, John?"

"Blood's thicker than water Danny. I'm with my brother," Baker flatly stated.

Danny removed John Baker from the offices and put him on the docks with his brother.

The beginning of the end for Greene's I.L.A. career came when stevedore manager Sigvald Refsnes returned to the docks, a year after losing his leg in a suspicious accident. Refsnes was a Norwegian merchant fleet captain who settled in Cleveland. He married Plain Dealer journalist Faith Corrigan.

When Refsnes heard of Greene's building fund shakedown operation and arrangements with Best Labor Service, he was furious. He informed his wife who fired off a letter to the Plain Dealer's managing editor, Ted Princiotto.

Memo to Ted:

I have been informed by a reliable source of a situation on the docks here in Cleveland which warrants investigation. A company called Best Labor Service, Inc. with offices at 3030 Woodland Ave. . . supplies longshoremen to the stevedoring companies. The men are hired daily since the requirements for their services vary according to the work—20 one day 50 the next. They are paid by the stevedoring the regular longshoreman's rate which I believe is close to $3 an hour. However, the checks are delivered to an agent of Best Labor which is entitled to cash them. The workers get $1.25 an hour of which 17 cents is charged as a fee. The rest goes to Best Labor. The workers are mostly Negroes, many illiterate and falling under the heading of "moving meat." They have no idea how much money they are really entitled to and that the papers they sign give Best Labor the right to this exhorbitant fee. Cleveland Stevedore has a contract with the union to get all their labor through the union and the rumor on the docks is that Danny Greene, the I.L.A. head here is behind Best Labor Service since the workers are union members. On the books, Greene gets $6,000 a year salary from the Union but he drives a new Cadillac automobile and displays other material forms of wealth. . .

I hear the Cleveland Stevedore Co. is beginning to supply the men with their check stubs so that they will know just how *much they made. This needs confirmation. The hourly scale for longshoremen is $2.68 an hour. By contract with the I.L.A., laborers must be hired through the union which means calling Danny Greene each evening. Men from the Best Labor outfit show up for the jobs while the union hall. . . has men sitting around waiting for jobs. The only way the Best Labor outfit could learn about the jobs is through Daniel Greene. . . You will be supplied with a list of the laborers involved in the next week.*

Faith

Ted Princiotto assigned an aggressive, young reporter named Sam Marshall to investigate. Six weeks of anonymous phone calls, secret meetings and undercover work were capped with signed affidavits from a score of fed-up but nervous longshoremen.

"Why was it necessary to work for nothing on the grain boats?" Marshall inquired of several of the men. From each, he received the same answer.

"Well, if I didn't work grain boats for nothing I wouldn't have been hired the next day or it would have caused some sort of friction on the job," one replied.

"If I wanted to work, I had to work the grain boats or I wouldn't be hired for any other work," another explained.

Greene was quick to boldly defend himself blaming his problems on dissident union members.

"The members have volunteered to donate all their grain boat checks if they want to offset the deficit created by our building program," he told Marshall. "If they wanted their money they could have it. You've been talking to a few dissidents. We have the program posted on the bulletin board."

He also denied that members had to work free on the grain boat to be eligible for regular paying work.

"Most certainly not. We've spent money to set up a system to insure that all available work is equally distributed. Those are all dissident members," Greene insisted.

Marshall conducted hundreds of interviews and spoke with shipping company officials.

"I've been aware of what's going on but I couldn't get anyone's ear, and I couldn't prove it", one stevedore boss complained. "No one ever had these problems in the fifty years of relations before Danny Greene took over. He's intimidated them to the point where nobody would say anything, but apparently the Plain Dealer has broken through. Someone ought to go to jail for this. They're exploiting the common working man and now these poor guys are having trouble making a living."

U.S. attorneys had heard enough and obtained a court order requiring Greene to surrender all of the I.L.A.'s financial records. Court officers tried to serve the subpoena but Danny could not be located. The next day in a surprise move, Danny called a special membership meeting. The dock workers responded with a record turnout in which Greene made a brief appearance, maintaining his innocence with even these men, the victims of his own greed. He went so far as to place blame on the membership for failing to bring forward their dissatisfaction and even denied knowing of the grain boat practice.

"If you don't want the grain boat operation by the union, speak up," Danny told them.

Immediately after the meeting, Greene was served with the subpoena for the court records. Later, in an interview with Sam Marshall, Danny defended the surprise meeting as "routine," and denied seeking a vote of confidence.

"Sure I rule with an iron hand, but that hand is with society and the port, not against them," he maintained.

But reporter Sam Marshall was as unrelenting as a Terrier after a rat. Despite the cautions of Princiotto and other Plain Dealer managers, he pressed on with the expose. The coverage won the praise of union members, city officials and stevedore officials.

"I am hopeful these matters will be thoroughly investigated by the appropriate authorities. Much recognition should go to the Plain Dealer for uncovering this situation which has plagued our port," one stevedore boss commented.

Danny's troubles had just begun. After receiving copies of Marshall's articles, an investigation was ordered by the I.L.A. international president. Danny's frustration got the best of him and he threatened Marshall.

"Sam we know you have a lovely wife and four beautiful children. I'd hate to see anything happen to them."

Marshall was frightened but never went to the police. In thirteen years of newspaper work, he had developed some of his own contacts on the other side. He made a phone call to Pasquale "Pat" Feruccio, a member of the Pittsburgh Mafia stationed in Canton, Ohio. Reportedly Feruccio contacted Cleveland mob chief John Scalish and informed him that a friend had been threatened. The next day Scalish had a message delivered to Danny.

"If anything happens to Sam Marshall or his family, you're gone."

Later, Danny telephoned Marshall to apologize.

"Sam, what in the hell did I say?" Greene asked, sounding genuinely confused.

"About what Danny?"

"Sam, I don't know what I said but please don't take it the wrong way. I'd never do anything to harm your family."

With that, Danny passed off the threat as mere misunderstanding. He was quite believable at explaining his behavior as having been misinterpreted. By then a large number of I.L.A. members filed the following petition with the national union:

We, the undersigned members of Local 1317, do hereby petition the president and executive board of the International Longshoremen's Association to place our local in trusteeship immediately, so we can hold a free election for leadership of our choice. Further we ask the international president and his executive board to send a representative from the international office to our local's membership for the purpose of discussing in detail each one of the points outlined in the attached report. Finally we ask the international president and his executive board to act at once as we, the undersigned, are fearful of other unions' attempts to take over this work which is our livelihood and so much of which has already been lost to neighboring, non-ILA ports through our leadership's unlawfully called strikes, slowdowns and through a reign of fear and treason to their own union brothers.

Wearing a confident smile, a conservative brown suit with his dia-mond-studded I.L.A. lapel-pin, and carrying several small, manila files, Danny Greene greeted Sam Marshall at Federal District Court. He continued to maintain that his problems were the result of "a few dissident I.L.A. members."

"The records are all there, Sam," he said shaking hands with the lone newspaperman who had brought him so much trouble.

Danny had grown skilled in the use of publicity in battle. His charming personality and natural talent for rhetoric were an effective combination. Danny was quite cunning in this regard. But Danny was not only street smart. As a child, he shunned school books, but instead sought to learn from books about great leaders, politics and history. With all of the reading Danny had done in his life, he had become sur-prisingly well-educated. But Sam Marshall knew better. Greene's assurance that "the records were all there" sounded convincing in the newspapers, but Danny hadn't even provided a fraction of the files that were subpoenaed.

Joining U.S. attorneys in the investigation of Greene were the U.S. Labor Department, the Federal Bureau of Investigation, the National Labor Relations Board and the Internal Revenue Service. Also aiding the effort was the Organized Crime and Racketeering Section of the U.S. Justice Department. They were enjoying national recognition for their success in the investigation of the International Brotherhood of Teamsters. As a result of that probe, national presi-dent James Hoffa and over one-hundred-fifty union officials were convicted of racketeering.

The dock investigators made numerous findings in the days that followed. The case against Greene took off after they searched his office. They discovered substantial financial records that Danny had refused to produce. Evidence showed that Danny failed to pay any contributions to the welfare system. After weeks of review by special auditors it was revealed that Greene had a very simple, though illegal method of operating his union's finances.

"We have found no records of any separate funds in the financial records we have gone through," a U.S. attorney reported. "Greene apparently operated everything from one fund."

Investigators made another startling discovery in Greene's office.

Part of Danny's original refurbishing of the union hall included an elaborate system of tiny, hidden microphones that he had secretly installed during two nights. The bugs were secreted in strategic locations and wired into phone lines to give Danny full coverage of conversations in the lobby, the meeting room, and the parking lot. Even the bathroom was bugged. The control panel which had recording capabilities was located in Danny's office, concealed behind a secret sliding panel. A stack of ten twelve-inch tapes sat nearby.

Sam Marshall was on hand for a demonstration of the eavesdropping system by local interim officer Chauncey Baker.

"You're on this tape Sam," Baker informed Marshall. "In a telephone conversation."

Danny had more problems. The day after the eavesdropping equipment was discovered, someone fired several, small-caliber shots into his home. Though it was 11:00 P.M., Danny was supposedly downtown meeting with his attorney. His wife Nancy and their two young daughters were home.

A reporter interviewed a frightened Nancy Greene about the incident.

"I went back downstairs to watch television. At first I thought it was just something happening outside. Danny has gotten other threats, but nothing like this has ever happened before. I was so upset last night, I couldn't even write down for the police what happened."

Only Danny's German Shepherd heard the shots and the glass breaking. The dog's barking sent Mrs. Greene to investigate and call the police who found the bullet holes.

"How is Danny doing?" the reporter asked.

"His Irish is up and he's fighting for his job," she said.

"What happens if he doesn't get it back?"

"He might lead a normal life then."

The next day, the same reporter telephoned Danny to interview him about the shooting.

By now Greene was feeling the heat of the dock investigation. And the shooting of his house didn't help matters.

"Why don't you ask that crusading newspaper of yours that prints only one slant of a story," Danny growled. "I'm sick of the racket. Consult my lawyers for any comment."

Danny hung up on the reporter but later prepared the following statement announcing his resignation from Local 1317 of the International Longshoremens Association. It was a typical display of Greene's effectiveness at rhetoric.

"Effective immediately, I have resigned as an officer and member of Local 1317, International Longshoremen's Association and as vice president of the Great LakesDistrict, International Longshoremen's Association. I have dropped any affiliation with the Longshoremen's Association and any connection with the labor movement. After nearly four years of devoting all my energies to get the dock workers in Cleveland a fair shake, I now find that my only compensation is headlines in the newspaper and bullets through my windows. Before March, 1961, I was a longshoreman working in the holds of ships when I was asked to take over this union and make something of it. Under my administration the union has moved from a tiny office in a dingy building to fine quarters near the waterfront where members could be proud to gather. The pay envelopes of Cleveland dock workers have increased 40% and $200,000 in welfare funds have been accumulated to care for the future and security of the men. Winos and drifters have disappeared from the waterfront. Criminals and pilferers have been dismissed. Decent men supporting families have taken their place. Experienced men now have job protection instead of depending upon the whim of a foreman for employment."

In the end, the multi-agency investigation produced enough evidence to indict Greene for embezzling roughly $35,000 from the I.L.A. and for falsifying union records. The case took on some interesting twists with Greene faring relatively well.

In 1966, he was convicted of three counts of embezzling $11,500 and two counts of falsifying records. He was sentenced to five years in prison but the sentence was suspended, apparently because it was his first offense. Greene appealed, and in 1968 the conviction was overturned by the U.S. Sixth Circuit Court of Appeals, on a technicality. In 1970, the case was disposed of when prosecutors agreed to drop felony embezzlement charges. In exchange, Danny plead guilty to two misdemeanor charges of falsifying union records. He was fined $10,000 and barred from working in any union or labor related business for five years.

Perhaps Danny was enjoying some protection from the F.B.I. as a result of his growing status as a confidential informant. He paid only a fraction of the fine and was never imprisoned.

Chapter 12

Alexander Birnstein was born in 1907 in the town of Lemes in a section of Austria-Hungary that went to Czechoslovakia under the Versailles Treaty. Youngest of three children, he was brought to the United States at the age of one month. From New York City, the family moved to Cleveland, Ohio, settling in the lower Woodland Avenue district.

Like many immigrant families, the Birnsteins "Americanized" their surname. In this case to Birn. Alexander's name was abbreviated to an English translation of Zander. But the Italian and Jewish neighbors took to calling the boy "Shondor," and that pronunciation stuck.

Like most immigrants, the Birn family struggled to earn a living in the new world. Like many immigrants during Prohibition, they turned to bootlegging, taking in a small still from Big Joe Lonardo to supplement their income and better provide for their children.

In November of 1920, Shondor's mother was tending to the 10-gallon still in the their apartment when a faulty gas connection caused an explosion. Scalding mash spewed out and flames engulfed the young mother's clothing. She ran outside screaming where a passing motorist helped extinguish the flames and drove the young woman to the hospital. Horribly burned over 75% of her body, she died the next morning.

Shondor was thirteen when he lost his mother so tragically. Like Danny Greene at Parmadale, Shondor was sheltered for a time in the old Jewish Orphanage where he met many friends. He grew up quickly taking on a job as a newspaper boy during the tough newspaper circulation wars. As a student, Shondor excelled at athletics, especially baseball and swimming. On the streets he developed a reputation among the neighborhood kids as a fighter, proving himself worthy with his fists in numerous tangles with street thugs. He learned quickly to apply the Old Testament justice of "an eye for an eye."

Shondor was drafted by E. 55th Street and Woodland mob leader Maxie Diamond who was associated with Bill Presser. For a time, the newspapers called Diamond "Cleveland's Number One Racketeer."

Birn became a ranking member of Diamond's gang during the battles for control of the city's dry cleaners and launderers. It was at roughly this time that Shondor changed his last name to Birns, to isolate his family from the embarrassment of his involvement with criminals. Then the real tangles with the law began: a stolen car conviction and an assault rap in which Birns broke the jaw of a motorist who had taken too long to make his turn in front of Shondor.

With eighteen arrests in a twelve-year period, Shondor was on his way to notoriety in northeast Ohio. He glowed in his fame, enjoying the attention in an almost endearing, pathetic manner. But he developed a knack for beating the charges. In that same time period, he was successfully prosecuted only twice. At age nineteen, Birns was convicted of auto theft and served two years in prison. In 1933, he was convicted of bribery and served sixty days and paid a $500 fine. After a half dozen appearances in court, a prosecutor remarked," it is time the courts put away this man whose reputation is one of rampant criminality." At the time, Birns was only in his twenties.

One of Birns' most serious arrests was for the 1934 murder of a bouncer at the Euclid Avenue Keystone Club. Shondor was sitting at the Keystone with two of his E. 55th Street and Woodland Avenue gangster buddies when he arose to fetch some cigars from his overcoat which he had checked in the coat room. The coatroom girl refused to give Birns access to his coat because he could not produce his check. Apparently he had misplaced it. Over her objections Shondor entered the coat room.

"Hey you can't come in here!" the girl insisted, blocking Shondor's path.

"Get out of the way," he warned shoving her aside. As the girl ran from the coatroom, Shondor retrieved some cigars from his coat and returned to his table. He had two more drinks and smoked one cigar.

"C'mon let's get outta here," he suggested. The men arose and went to get their coats.

This time the coatroom girl was ready. She had summoned Rudy Duncan, the bouncer who also happened to be her live-in boyfriend. She told him about the incident with Birns. Duncan, a thirty-six-year-old ex-boxer with arrests in Pittsburgh, Buffalo and Cleveland, had experienced previous run-ins with Shondor Birns and his buddies. When the girl refused to give Birns his coat sans a receipt, he shoved her aside and reached for his coat. Duncan came up behind him.

"What are you doing in here?" he demanded in a menacing tone.

Birns muttered something and the two lunged at each other.

"So, you're trying to get tough are you Rudy?" Birns warned as he pulled a revolver from his waistband while struggling to hold Duncan back with one hand. He raised the gun to hit Duncan in the head. But four cocktails had slowed Birns and Duncan got hold of the weapon with one hand as he pulled his own pistol. Two shots went off. Birns was hit in the shoulder and one of his friends was shot in the leg. Duncan ordered Birns' crew out of the bar at gunpoint.

When the police arrived they found Shondor in his car ready to pull away while holding a bloody handkerchief to his shoulder. They searched his car and confiscated the revolver which he had placed in the glove box. He denied ownership of the gun and would not tell who shot him. The police drove him to the hospital.

After two days, Shondor checked himself out of the hospital. He was well on his way to a full recovery when he was arrested and charged with carrying a concealed weapon.

During the trial, Birns testified that whoever came up behind him in the cloakroom had the gun. He didn't see his assailant.

"Well, it was a small room, wasn't it," the assistant prosecutor asked him. "Can't you tell us who that man was?"

"No, I was shot and hit over the nose and in the head," Birns insisted. You know how it is when you're in a fight. Blood was coming down over my eyes and I couldn't see."

Shondor refused to identify Duncan as the man who shot him. He even denied knowing Duncan at all. Perhaps he was laying the groundwork for his own justice. And admitting that he knew who shot him could create grounds for a motive should some harm befall Duncan. Likewise, Rudy Duncan's recollection of the incident was so poor that he wasn't even called as a witness. Maybe he had similar plans in mind.

Shondor was convicted of attempting to bribe a witness in the case. While serving his sentence in the Warrensville Workhouse, he granted his first newspaper interview. Shondor told the reporter that he was serving his time happily and enjoying the hard work. In the years to come, he became close with many of the city's newspaper reporters and could be found chatting with one over a cocktail, courtesy of Shon, of course. He was an excellent source of news tips.

A few weeks after the trial, two-well dressed men wearing white cotton gloves loitered outside the Uptown Theater at E. 105th Street and Saint Clair Avenue. It was evening. Two more men waited in the parking lot in an automobile.

Inside the theater, Rudy Duncan and his eleven-year-old son, Stanley were watching the end of a movie. After the show, Duncan took the boy to a store next to the theater and bought him some candy. Then they headed for their car.

Duncan tooled the car out of the lot and headed west on St Clair as he and his boy chatted about the show. Moments later Rudy noticed two cars coming up fast; one from behind and one on his left. The car on the left held a man standing on the running board. He had a handkerchief tied about his face. Duncan slammed on his brakes and pushed the boy out of the car.

"Run! Run Stanley!" he yelled. The boy dashed out of the street onto the sidewalk but then stopped and turned around.

Duncan stepped on the gas but it was too late. The two cars were right on him. Several men let loose a barrage of pistol-fire, then sped off. Duncan's car drifted aimlessly to the right, bounced off the curb then rolled to a stop. Duncan's son came running to his father's aid.

"Daddy! Daddy!", the boy screamed.

The boy peered inside the car. It was too late. Blood was pumping out of two bullet holes in Duncan's chest and he was taking his last labored breath. His murder went officially unsolved, but Birns remained a prime suspect. An eye for an eye. Nobody pushed Shon around.

Chapter 13

During the late thirties, Shondor Birns became heavily involved in protecting whorehouses or "vice resorts" as they were dubbed by the newspapers. It was quite fun for him and all the girls liked him. He operated freely and with the blessing of local Mafiosi whom he had grown up with. Many of Shondor's clients were judges, politicians and ranking police officers. They would be important contacts for Birns in the future, as he would be for them.

In 1938, Birns visited Canada for vacation. When he reentered the United States he was questioned briefly about criminal history and answered honestly. It was a grave error he always regretted. At the time, Shondor knew nothing of the Immigration Act of 1917 which required any alien convicted of a crime of moral turpitude to gain permission prior to entering or leaving the country. It would take a couple of years for the paperwork to catch up.

In the meantime, Safety Director Eliot Ness completed a long investigation into the numbers racket. Among those indicted were Birns, Angelo Lonardo and Maishe Rockman. Convictions cost most of them two years in prison.

◆　　◆　　◆

World War II had a sobering effect on La Cosa Nostra members and their associates. Italy was now at war with their beloved America. Their sons served in the armed forces and a hunger for respectability began. In 1942, Cleveland had the lowest crime rate in its history. That year, Birns was arrested on a deportation warrant based on the auto theft and bribery convictions. Two months later, his attorney was successful in getting him released on bond. But officials were deter-mined to keep Shondor locked up. A wartime presidential order was issued charging Birns as an enemy alien, and he was interned at McAlester, Oklahoma. He was deeply offended. He had always con-sidered himself a patriotic American. Upon his release in 1944, Shondor returned to Cleveland and was well known by police, judges and the public. He was "Cleveland's Hood," and many sympathized with him in what was seen as a vendetta.

Birns told people he was trying to go straight when he opened his Ten-Eleven Club at 1011 Chester Avenue. Serving excellent food, the restaurant was favored by local and out-of-town big shots. Police and newspaper reporters ate and drank on the house. When the tragic East Ohio Gas explosion killed 134 persons and left thousands homeless in 1944, Birns kept the Ten-Eleven Club open 24 hours-a-day, feeding policemen, firemen and rescue workers for free.

During the forties, Shondor became involved with local Mafiosi like Angelo Lonardo, who had already taken over black policy and clearinghouse—illegal lottery operations. Birns was determined that as long as he was alive, he would be the big white man in this increas-ingly black racket.

"The niggers have the idea since they organized clearing house and policy, it should belong to them. If you don't keep the niggers in line, the first thing you know they will be running the city."

One of the best known of the black, numbers operators was Donald King, the future fight promoter. In the mid-sixties, Donald "the Kid" King and his partner Virgil Ogletree were reportedly grossing $15,000 daily on policy. King gained prominence among the other operators in 1954, after he thwarted a robbery of one of his gambling houses, killing one of the stick-up men. The shooting was ruled justifiable.

Apparently, the shooting bolstered King's self-confidence because he began holding out on the protection money being paid to Birns, Lonardo and their associates. One morning in 1957, an explosion ripped apart the front porch of King's house. Uninjured, he went to the police accusing Birns of ordering the bombing. Largely on his tes-timony, Birns and the others were indicted. A few weeks later, Birns and his boys tried to dissuade King from testifying with a blast from a 12-gauge shotgun. Several pellets of shot found a home in the back of his head, but Donald the Kid survived to testify.

When the trial began, King was cast as the star witness in the trial. The judge and jury had difficulty understanding King and newspaper reporters quickly dubbed him "The Talker" because of his rapid, inarticulate speech. In the end, Birns and the others were acquitted.

In 1966, King again surfaced significantly in the news when he stomped to death one his employees holding out on a $600 payment. When police arrested him, he said, "you don't have to handcuff me, I'm Donald King."

Despite a significant campaign of threats, hush money, and uncooperative witnesses, King was ultimately convicted of second-degree murder. He was sentenced to life in prison. But before being shipped off to the Ohio Penitentiary, King's conviction was lessened to manslaughter by Judge Hugh Corrigan. The reduction was done absent representation by the prosecutor's office and without a court stenographer. Only King's attorney was present. Donald "the Kid" King was released from prison after serving only four years.

In later years, author Jack Newfield in his book *Only in America—The Life and Crimes of Don King*, reported on allegations that Corrigan had been influenced by organized crime. Newfield pointed out an F.B.I. memo which accused Corrigan of receiving $6,000 for a favor.

Despite opposition from the Mafia, Donald "the Kid" stayed busy in the numbers racket. He invested some of his numbers profits in the New Corner Tavern where he brought in entertainers like Errol Garner, B.B. King and Jonah Jones.

◆   ◆   ◆

At age 40, Shondor Birns was still seeking respectability through his popular Alhambra Restaurant where judges and politicians dined. During the early morning hours, Birns would often send food over to the nearby Fifth District Police Station for the officers working the late shift. Though Birns was pursued for decades by law enforcers, he seemed to respect, even admire the city's men in blue.

Once when he was under 24-hour surveillance, Birns was leaving a Cleveland Indians baseball game. He happened to notice the two detectives assigned to follow him and flagged them over. The officers agreed to drive him to his next destination. When the officers were reprimanded by a supervisor, Shondor intervened on their behalf.

"I knew it was near their shift change and I just wanted to give the fellas a hand so they wouldn't lose me in the crowd. And that way it would be easier for the next shift to pick me up."

Birns was sincere! Though he was aggressively pursued virtually his whole life by law enforcers, the last thing he wanted was to get a detective or patrolman in hot water with his supervisor.

Chapter 14

On a peaceful spring morning in 1968, the quiet was shattered as a foursome of business associates and friends approached the 16th hole at Orchard Hills Golf Course in rural northeast Ohio. One of the men was just about to tee off when a shot echoed through the countryside. A slug from an assassin's rifle found its mark.

"I've been shot!" the golfer screamed, clutching at his back.

Six more shots rang out in rapid succession and four more struck the golfer as he collapsed. Two rounds furrowed into the green as the other golfers raced back to the clubhouse to summon help. A courageous, young groundskeeper ran to the man's aid but it was too late.

Perino DiGravio, better known as Pete, was a handsome, well-known businessman with a successful, short term loan operation headquartered in Little Italy. Fastidious in personal health and appearance, the blue-eyed DiGravio dressed well and rarely smoked or drank. He jogged daily.

DiGravio's lending business was based on a short term, simple "6 for 5" system in which he was paid back six dollars for every five dollars loaned. Customers late with their payments were charged 5% "vigorish," a rackets term for an extra assessment not deducted from the principal.

DiGravio was closely associated with local Mafiosi, including Scalish lieutenant Jack Licavoli. One of the partners in his MDM Investment Company was John "Curly" Montana, a known mob figure and alleged hitman. DiGravio was an independent businessman who operated free of Mafia control or influence. He insisted that his loans never resulted in violence to anyone and that he had prominent backers including former heavyweight boxing champion Rocky Marciano, with whom he was very close.

Though many of his customers included doctors, lawyers and other legitimate clientele, DiGravio catered to gamblers and other persons unlikely to be accepted for a conventional loan.

By 1968, DiGravio's operation had picked up considerably. He was well-liked and respected by his borrowers. If one of them died before his loan was repaid, DiGravio sent flowers to the funeral and never approached the family to collect the unpaid balance. But for the likes of the Cleveland Mafia, DiGravio was becoming too successful. They wanted in. Reportedly, members of the Scalish family approached DiGravio and demanded an off-the-top cut of 10%. He refused.

A few weeks before his murder, DiGravio was interviewed by a journalist from the Cleveland Press. The reporter asked about the effects of new federal legislation which would prohibit operations such as DiGravio's, and also about a rumor of mob involvement in his company.

"Just because we may be tough Italians doesn't mean we are Mafia-connected," he insisted. . . "I have enough problems with this new law. I need the Mafia like I need cancer."

Pete DiGravio's killer or killers were never identified. The most persistent motive for his murder was his public disdain of the Mafia, and his refusal to cut them in on his lucrative, money lending operation. Once again, the Cleveland Mafia had proven themselves a force to reckoned with.

The same scene was played out a few years later when mob enforcer David Perrier began attracting attention in local bars, getting drunk and getting into fights. On one occasion, he started bad-mouthing Jack Licavoli. A friend of Licavoli's was present and spoke up. Perrier slapped him across the face.

Several days later, realizing what he had done, Perrier met with Licavoli, got down on his knees and begged his forgiveness. But the damage was already done. The reputation of the Cleveland mob, particularly that of Licavoli, was on the line. Punishment had to be swift with those who so blatantly disrespected La Cosa Nostra.

A week later, Perrier's body was found in rural northeast Ohio. He had been shot numerous times in the head. Cleveland mobsters had sent a message. They would not tolerate being embarrassed or challenged.

Chapter 15

By 1960, the hauling and disposal of rubbish was becoming an attractive business. As private and public industry continued to grow, so did the tons of waste they produced. Efficient and relatively clean dumpsters, roll-off containers and off-site options were replacing overflowing, 55-gallon drums and back rooms filled with cardboard boxes of putrid garbage awaiting pick-up. Until then, rubbish haulers often carried sticks to fend off hungry rats. Though the nature of solid waste disposal was not appealing to the average businessman, the future for rubbish hauling looked promising. As business increased, small waste hauling firms opened. Their owners were typically tough, street-educated, entrepreneurs with ambition. There was bound to be conflict. And since there was money to be made, the Mafia was bound to be part of it.

In New York City, waste hauling companies had already been infiltrated by the Mafia. Joseph Messina was originally from New York City where he had relatives—the Lomangino brothers—in rubbish hauling. In 1968, Messina moved to Cleveland. He became associated with Frank Brancato through his friendship with Carmen Semenoro, a New Jersey mob enforcer who relocated to Cleveland.

Within a short time, Semenoro became a protege to Brancato and was rumored to be the heir to "Uncle Frank's" Licatese Mafia faction operation. Semenoro's boastful nature got him in trouble before he could inherit control of the small but mighty crew. Brancato warned him to keep his mouth shut, but Semenoro found pleasure in bragging about his current and past mob accomplishments.

Perhaps it was Semenoro's loose tongue that brought he and Brancato federal indictments for extortion. The F.B.I. alleged that the two were shaking down a modular homes dealer in Youngstown, Ohio. It was shortly after the indictments were handed down that a mob executioner crept into the darkness outside Semenoro's apartment. The assassin was armed with a 12-gauge shotgun loaded with heavy buckshot. When he saw his target he fired several blasts through the window, striking Semenoro in the head and killing him instantly. Eventually the charges against Brancato were dropped in U.S. District Court.

Shortly after Joseph Messina started a small waste hauling service called A-1 Rubbish Disposal, he began getting late night visits from men in expensive cars. Messina was receiving instructions from James "Jimmy Brown" Failla, an up-and-coming power in a Nassau County crew of New York's Gambino crime family. Failla was a business agent for a New York rubbish hauler union. With Mafia help, Messina was to organize the various waste haulers in the Cleveland area. Messina was the choice for the assignment because he was familiar with the industry through his cousins. Messina used to ride on their garbage trucks as a boy. Failla had cleared the way for Messina through Frank Brancato.

Meanwhile, several prominent and legitimate businessmen had already begun organizing the Cleveland rubbish haulers by founding the Cleveland Solid Waste Trade Guild. The idea was to eliminate under-cutting and price fixing, and guarantee a fair piece of the waste disposal profits for all involved.

Frank Brancato was finding that Joe Messina was not the man for the job. Messina had become side-tracked by making his own rubbish hauling firm a priority and was using Brancato's name to steal customers. So Brancato moved Danny Greene into the job.

"If the others don't join, we will follow their trucks and take away their stops," Danny was heard to suggest. "We'll offer to pick up for less and take away their business at the cheapest price—and knock them out of the box. . . There are a lot of ways we can do this and then we'll split up the stops and give them to guild members. . ."

Danny denied the statement when he was interviewed by a reporter.

"Some of the 'big guys' came to me and said they had a multitide of problems," Greene explained. "They wanted to know if I would help them form a trade organization. I did a little research and learned that it is a dog-eat-dog business with every hauler working around the clock to steal the other guy's stops. . . Knowing the group had made several abortive attempts to organize, I thought I could be of help and took the job."

When the reporter asked who the "big guys" were, Danny declined to name them.

One of Danny Greene's closest allies in the Cleveland Solid Waste Trade Guild was a friend, Mike Frato. A barrel-chested, three-hundred-pound man, Frato was called "Big Mike" by his many friends. Despite his size, he was soft-spoken with an engaging personality. He loved children, fathering fourteen with three different wives and hoped some day to open a home for neglected boys. He was a hard-working, successful businessman, but a nagging gambling habit kept him in debt.

Mike Frato got his start in rubbish hauling in 1957 with $700 and one truck. In the following years he was able to expand to eighteen trucks with a gross income of $1 million a year. He was a legitimate businessman who protested when he realized that Danny was bringing mob involvement and strong-arm tactics to the guild. So Frato left the Cleveland Solid Waste Trade Guild and started his own organization—Cuyahoga County Refuse Haulers Association. Other rubbish haulers left the Solid Waste Trade Guild and Greene's racket fell apart.

"The guild was a beautiful thing at first," Frato told a reporter. "But the wrong people took control. I didn't need it anymore. You might say I was expelled."

"Who got control of the guild," the reporter asked.

"I don't want to talk about it."

Chapter 16

On October 31, 1971, a squad of Cleveland Heights detectives watched as young ghosts and goblins completed their joyous tour of the city's side streets. With shotguns at the ready, the officers concealed themselves in the vicinity of the city hall and service department buildings. The detectives chatted and joked in their two-man unmarked cars as they continuously scanned the area for anything or anyone suspicious. Earlier in the day, an anonymous caller informed a police dispatcher that someone was going to blow up the city hall.

A half mile down busy Mayfield Road, toward Little Italy, is the intersection of Coventry Road. Coventry Village, a popular entertainment district, was a sixties hang-out for hippies and bikers and home to a jumble of head shops, unique gift boutiques, ethnic restaurants and saloons. On the northwest corner of the intersection sat Swan's Service Station in which Mike Frato was a partner. On the southeast corner was a three story brick building which housed the office of Frato's Cuyahoga County Refuse Haulers Association. It was at the Swan service station that Frato parked his Cadillac when he visited his office.

At 12:30 A.M. it happened. The detectives were jolted. A few seconds later it was over as they headed in the direction of the explosion. About ninety seconds later they located the source of the blast. Calls began flooding the police switchboard as fire equipment was dispatched.

The outside of Swan's Service Station, damage from a bomb was obvious. Numerous windows in nearby buildings were blown out. Inside the service station detectives found a smoldering, badly damaged Cadillac. A few feet away they made a gruesome discovery. It was the body of a man lying face down against a nearby wall. Judging from the vicious loss of his arms, face and chest, he had been the focus of the powerful blast and died instantly.

The detectives ran a computer check on the license plate of the Cadillac and found that it was listed to Michael Frato. But the dead body was not his. Frato had been playing cards in an office across the street when his car was bombed. The police cordoned off the area and began investigating. The Bureau of Alcohol, Tobacco and Firearms, Cleveland Police Intelligence Unit and the Coroner's Office were called in to assist.

◆   ◆   ◆

Art Snepeger had been an all-purpose errand man, loyal to Danny Greene since their days on the railroads and docks. For the rubbish guild, Art was responsible for urging non-members to join. He had experience with dynamite, occasionally working with cement contractors to blow out tree stumps. He handled some bombings for Greene, but when Danny asked Art to commit murder, he misjudged his friend.

In September, Snepeger fixed a bomb on Frato's car but had second thoughts. He had grown up with Frato in the Woodland Avenue, "bloody corner", neighborhood and was already too involved. Danny was going too far. Snepeger removed the bomb from Frato's car, telephoned Big Mike and informed him of Greene's plan.

Several days later, Snepeger received a phone call from Sgt. Kovacic of the Cleveland Police Intelligence Unit. Kovacic was working on the bombing of a grocery store and wanted to question Snepeger. He knew Snepeger was involved but had no evidence so he bluffed, threatening to charge him with arson. The bluff worked infinitely better than Kovacic had predicted, the result being a forty-page statement by Snepeger regarding the criminal activities of Danny Greene and several other Cleveland gangsters. Snepeger explained how Greene's inner circle of longshoremen muscled, threatened and beat dock workers.

"If someone complained, they'd get a beating. If someone went to the police, they'd get a beating. Even if one of them just said something bad about Danny, we'd rough him up."

"Was there a name for this group?" Kovacic asked.

"Yeah, the grievance committee."

Most interesting to Kovacic was Snepeger's revelation that Greene was indeed an F.B.I. informant. Kovacic had suspected the same for several years.

A few weeks after Snepeger talked to Kovacic, Danny contacted Art, demanding that he return to work for him. During the evening of October 31st, Snepeger was on his way out of the house when he spoke briefly with his girlfriend about the situation.

"I've gotta go back to work for Danny cause I'm dead if I don't. And I'm dead if I do," he tried to explain without revealing too much.

It was the last time the girl ever saw Art alive. Shortly after the Cleveland Heights bombing, police identified the disfigured body from Swan's Service Station as that of Snepeger. The police and Bureau of Alcohol, Tobacco and Firearms agents located Snepeger's car near the bombing scene. Inside they found a remote control for an electric dog training collar and various bomb parts.

That Snepeger died while planting a bomb on Frato's car by order of Danny Greene was certain. Theories as to why the bomb went off prematurely were conflicting. Some investigators felt certain that the explosion was an accident caused by a radio signal, possibly from a short-wave radio or passing police car. Snepeger's girlfriend was convinced that Art's death was a murder arranged by Shondor Birns and Danny Greene. Though the case was never officially solved, Sgt. Kovacic was told that Greene had waited at Snepeger's car while he planted the bomb. When Snepeger returned to the car, Greene told him that he wanted additional dynamite affixed to the bomb. When Snepeger went back to Frato's car, Greene pressed the button on the detonator. The likely motive: Greene had learned of the statement that Snepeger made to police.

Shortly after Snepeger's death, Frato received the following unsigned, threatening letter.

If there is anymore senseless violence by you three punks you will be annihilated. We did not build this town to have it destroyed. Believe it or not. The advice contained in this letter is being mailed to all three of you punks.

Authorities sought answers to numerous questions. Who sent the letters? Was it the Scalish Mafia family? Perhaps the local mobsters were concerned that more violence would bring unwanted heat from law enforcers. And who were the other two punks? Danny Greene and Joe Messina ?

Messina wasn't home when his wife received a phone call.

"Tell Joe to keep his nose clean. We can't protect him anymore."

Messina didn't need anymore warnings. He packed up and left town, never to return to Cleveland.

Mike Frato was nervous and began carrying a gun. But he was more concerned that his former best friend, Danny Greene, was out to kill him.

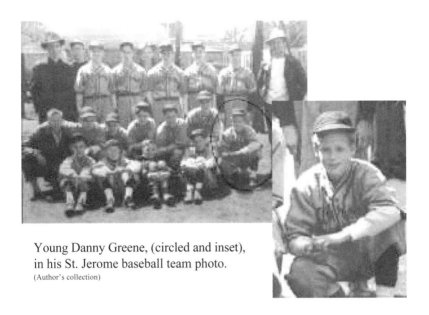

Young Danny Greene, (circled and inset),
in his St. Jerome baseball team photo.
(Author's collection)

The Collinwood 2-family house where Danny lived with his
grandfather. (Author's collection)

Danny, as he appeared in his Marine Corps induction photo.
(Courtesy of Military Personnel Records Center)

Danny Greene in his first known mug shot
(Courtesy of Cleveland Police Department)

James Licavoli, age 19.

(Author's collection)

James "Jack White" Licavoli being questioned by a
Congressional committee in the fifties.

(Courtesy of Cleveland State University)

Leo "Lips" Moceri, circa 1967.
(Author's Collection)

Danny Greene, circa 1966.
(Author's Collection)

Don King, famous boxing
promoter and former Cleveland
numbers racketeer. (Courtesy of Everett/
Cleveland State University)

Labor leaders Jimmy Hoffa (left)
and Babe Triscaro.

(Courtesy of Cleveland State University)

Frank Brancato, one of several senior mob figures who brought Danny Greene into the Mafia scene. (Cleveland Police photo)

Time out for the photographer. A group of Cleveland mob figures and their attorneys, circa 1960. Second from left is Angelo Lonardo. Third is Shondor Birns. (Author's Collection)

Danny being questioned by journalist Sam Marshall.

(Courtesy of Sam Marshall)

Pete DiGravio (right), operator of an independent and successful loan business, murdered by Mafia bullets. He is shown next to his close friend, boxing great Rocky Marciano. (Author's collection)

Collinwood Village: proud neighborhood for a proud Irishman. (Author's collection)

Headquarters for Local 1317 of the International Longshoremens Association as it appeared in the sixties. In the background is the old Cleveland stadium. (Courtesy of Cleveland State University)

The "Shape-up." Dock workers hoping for work that day gather outside Danny Greene's I.L.A. local. (Courtesy of Cleveland State University)

The remains of Greene's Collinwood apartment after it was bombed in
fulfillment of a murder contract left by Shondor Birns. Miraculously,
Danny and his girlfriend walked away with only minor injuries.
(Courtesy of Cleveland Police Department)

Shondor Birns in a 1957 mugshot. Notice the update
placed on the photo by a detective after Birns was
killed by a car bomb. (Author's collection)

Never publicity-shy, Danny Greene poses for a newspaper photographer next to his demolished apartment. (Courtesy of Cleveland State University - photo by Timothy Culek)

The car-bomb murder scene of Shondor Birns showing the windshield
which was blown up onto a fire escape. (Author's collection)

Close-up of Birns' remains - an upper torso (face down), and foot
(partially socked) with heel showing. (Author's collection)

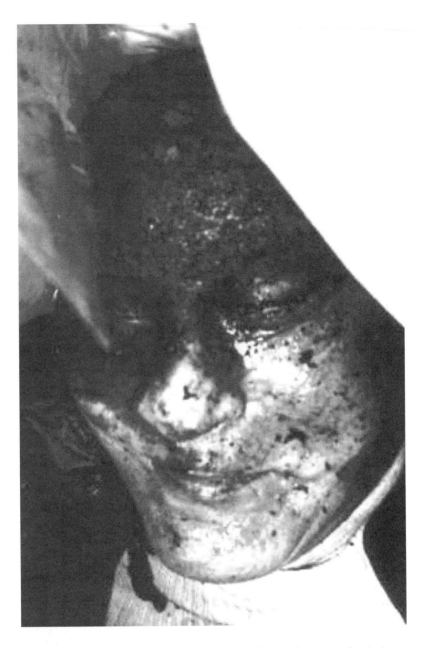

Birns' nose was broken when his body landed on the street after being blown out the top of his car. His hair was scorched off from the heat of the horrific blast. (Author's collection)

John Nardi, the union
official and reputed
mob boss candidate
who teamed up with
Danny Greene.

(Cleveland Police Museum)

Peter and Carmen Milano, boss and underboss of the Southern
California Mafia, and cousins-by- marriage to John Nardi.

(Author's collection)

A Celtic Club business card - green printing, of course, on a white background. (Author's collection)

Pasquale "Butchie" Cisternino, mob soldier who led the war against Danny Greene and John Nardi. (F.B.I. photo)

Feared Mafia enforcer Eugene "the Animal" Ciasullo pictured with legendary entertainer Sammy Davis Jr. at a Lake Tahoe, Nevada party celebrating Davis' 50th anniversary in show business. (Author's Collection)

Leo "Lips" Moceri, Mafia underboss killed by Nardi/Greene henchmen. Circa 1975. (Courtesy of the Cleveland Police Museum)

Tony Liberatore, union official and Mafia member. "Lib," as his friends and associates called him, supplied the back-up hit men in the Greene murder plot. (Author's collection)

Ronnie Carabbia, Cleveland Mafia figure from Youngstown, Ohio who, along with Ray Ferritto and Butchie Cisternino, would finally succeed in killing Greene. (F.B.I. photo)

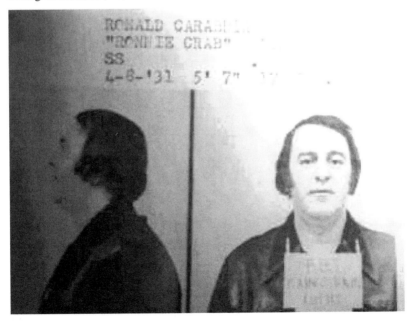

Chapter 17

Two patrolmen had just finished interviewing the victim of an assault at Saint Lukes Hospital emergency room and were heading out to their cruiser. They were pulling away from the parking spot when a Buick Riviera was driven urgently into the lot.

"There's something wrong with the passenger," one of the officers said motioning toward the Buick. The driver of the car parked, exited, glanced at the officers and hurried into the Emergency Room where he disappeared.

The officers pulled next to the Buick and got out to check the passenger, a large white man who was slumped against the door. Though dead or unconscious, the man's girth had kept him in a seated position with his head leaning halfway out the open window. Closer inspection by the officers revealed a bullet wound to the man's head and pools of blood on the seat and floor. The policemen ran into the emergency room.

"There's a guy shot in a car outside!" one of them shouted to a nurse hurrying toward them.

The public address system had suddenly come to life as a middle-aged, black female voice announced calmly, "Code Blue E.R. entrance. Code Blue E.R. entrance. Code Blue E.R. entrance." Personnel from various parts of the floor started rushing toward the emergency room. It was too late.

After homicide detectives arrived on the scene, the deceased passenger was identified as Mike Frato. The driver was a close friend. Later that afternoon detectives received an anonymous phone call stating "Mike Frato had his pistol out gunning for Danny Greene."

The investigation of Frato's death turned towards Greene who seemed to be mysteriously absent. Detectives checked all of his usual haunts to no avail. Two days went by then detectives received a phone call from Danny.

"I'm at the Concord Hotel in Painesville. I want to come in and straighten this matter out," Greene told them. The detectives made the forty-five minute trip to Painesville, arrested Danny and returned him for questioning. He was cooperative and made the following statement.

"About 10:30 in the morning I drove my three dogs to White City Beach like I do almost every day. I was there jogging and exercising my dogs when a car started driving slowly at me. The passenger shouted 'I've got you now you sonavabitch' and pointed a revolver at me. I recognized him as Mike Frato. He was about fifteen feet away and then he shot at me two times. I pulled out my gun and fired once then the car sped away. I didn't think that I killed him. I thought that I hit him in the shoulder. I thought somebody else might try to kill me so I went to Painesville."

Whether Frato shot at Greene to kill him or merely scare him was never determined. Suffice to say it was a sad turn of events. The two men were so close at one time that they named sons after each other. Later it was learned that Frato was armed and had an opportunity to kill Greene several weeks prior to the White City Beach shooting.

"I was within twenty feet of him," Frato confided to a friend. "I thought about doing it but I couldn't."

Ultimately, the case against Danny was thrown out before it went to trial.

"The evidence indicated that Frato was attempting to assassinate Danny Greene. . . in a struggle between the two for control of the rubbish hauling business," the judge commented.

Not long after the Frato shooting, Greene again found himself a target while jogging on White City Beach. A sniper, concealed several hundred feet away, fired several shots at Greene from a rifle. The man thought he would have an easy target as Greene jogged along with no cover. But instead of ducking to the ground, Danny pulled out his revolver and started shooting while running toward his would-be assassin, in complete disregard for his own safety. The tactic worked as the sniper fled and was never positively identified.

Later it would be learned that this was an attempt to fulfill the Greene murder contract left by Shondor Birns.

Chapter 18

With the backing of Frank Brancato, Danny Greene started Emerald Industrial Relations. For a hefty price, the labor consulting firm offered "protection" against union discord, supply problems and work stoppages. Most of the problems were manufactured by Greene. For instance, Greene was able to get a load of glass held up at a New York dock. Only until the construction firm came up with a $2,000 "consultation fee," did the glass find its way to Cleveland. Most companies paid up rather than suffer expensive delays.

Vincent "Fish" Cafaro, a Mafia turncoat explained why corruption of labor unions was a favored racket for the mob.

"We got our money from gambling, but our real power, our real strength, came from the unions. With the unions behind us, we could shut down the city, or the country for that matter, if we needed to get our way."

To promote Emerald Industrial Relations, Danny had specially-imprinted green-ink pens. He ordered them by the thousand and passed them out as gifts.

After a Dallas-based building firm complained about a ghost employee scam on their construction site, an investigation was begun by Cleveland Police Intelligence. The case took them to Dallas and St. Louis and back to Cleveland where Danny Greene's extortionist tactics had brought downtown construction almost to a halt. Investigators returned with numerous cardboard boxes of evidence. It looked like Danny Greene was again headed for some serious trouble with the law.

Affidavits were presented to a federal judge charging Greene with labor racketeering and violation of his parole, which prohibited him from working in the labor movement for another two years. It looked like an open and shut case until the judge, suddenly and without explanation, announced that he was dismissing the allegations.

It was a full year before investigators were told why their efforts were in vain.

"It's hard to say no to J. Edgar Hoover," the judge explained.

The information being supplied by Danny Greene was so valuable that it even warranted the protection of the F.B.I. director.

Chapter 19

By the seventies, Shondor Birns had mellowed, playing handball daily and spending several hours on lunch and a cocktail or two. He didn't want anymore trouble.

"Kid, I don't break any provisions of parole," he promised his young parole officer. "I'll tell you why. If I go back to jail, I'll die there."

Most often, Birns chose to lunch at the Theatrical, where he always sat at the end of the bar. Admirers, businessmen and friends stopped to say hello. Attorneys, judges and politicians paused from their lunches and busy conversations to wave, "Hi Shon."

Birns once told a reporter, "If I'm the city's biggest crook, why do they all want to be my friend? I'll tell you why. Most of them are worse than I am, and they know that I know. . ."

After lunch, Birns would head to the Silver Quill or Christie's Lounge and socialize while he nursed another cocktail. His most recent subject of choice was his upcoming retirement to Florida. But he still had some business to tend to.

Indeed, Birns was in his golden years and despite his love of the streets, he knew it was time to settle down. Financially he was set and he had spent too much time in jail late in life with recent bribery and perjury convictions. And there were some close calls.

Shondor had been suspected of two killings, including that of Mervin Gold. In the sixties Gold was being investigated for using stolen Canadian bonds to secure a bank loan. On July 8, 1963, he was found murdered and stuffed in the trunk of his car. He had been beaten, strangled with a clothesline and shot in the chest. A blanket was wrapped around his head. He was shot three more times in the skull.

If the motive for the killing was to silence Gold, it was unsuccessful. Anticipating an untimely demise, he left behind an affidavit claiming that Birns had given him the bonds. Gold's wife stated that her husband was on his way to meet with Birns the night he was murdered.

Amid aggressive accusations by police, Shondor insisted he had been dining on frog legs when Gold was killed. All concerned were shocked when Birns produced a shy, 24-year-old school teacher who confirmed his alibi claiming that she had been with Shon the whole night. She later married the charismatic hood.

By this time, Birns was beginning to have trouble overseeing the black numbers operators. What he needed was some muscle. Gutsy Danny Greene was just the man. For a relatively small cut of their profits, $1000 weekly, Birns had been serving as a peacemaker among the black, settling disputes that often resulted in stabbings and shootings. He also layed off or distributed big bets to other cities like Pittsburgh, so no single operator lost too much if a number came up.

During one of Danny's first assignments, he was supposed to toss a bomb at a dissident numbers man who was holding out on Shondor's protection money. Danny was by himself. He stopped a block down the street and pulled the igniter. But Greene was unfamiliar with the military type detonator. The fuse was burning faster than he had anticipated. Danny fumbled with the bomb and tried to throw it out the passenger window but it hit the door frame and bounced back in the car. Greene opened the door to escape. He just barely made it out of the car when the bomb exploded, blowing the roof off the car. Greene got up and walked away.

"The luck of the Irish," Danny would later say. His worst injury was to his right eardrum leaving him hard of hearing for life.

His story to the police was that somebody had driven by and thrown a bomb in his car.

It was about this time that Danny decided to open a cheat spot—an after hours drinking and gambling club—on the east side. He pitched the idea to Shondor Birns who agreed to loan Greene $70,000. Most of the investment money came from members of New York's Gambino family who were friends of Birns. Problems developed when Birns insisted that Greene hire a certain black man to handle some of the business at the club. The man turned out to be a drug dealer and decided to use some of the $70,000 to finance a drug deal on the side. Police were already investigating the man and a raid on his apartment resulted in him disposing of the cocaine by emptying it out a fourth-story window. To make matters worse, the club itself was raided only a day before it was to open.

Relations between the former Public Enemy Number One and ex-longshoreman turned sour. They blamed each other for the loss of the money and things began heating up. Shondor demanded that Greene pay back the loan so the Gambino mobsters could be repaid.

"Fuck 'em," Danny told Birns. "Tell 'em it was a gift."

As if Shondor didn't have enough problems to contend with, now a cocky, brazen young punk was going to take him for seventy Gs.

"That no good, fucking psychopath," Birns grumbled.

Shondor was already dealing with heavy opposition from a few black gangsters who wanted the old white guy out of their racket. Times were changing. Black racketeers had long been under the thumb of the more powerful and politically connected Mafiosi and their associates like Shondor. Now they were demanding their independence. Several close calls had made that clear. He bought a Doberman Pinscher to protect his home. It would have been a good time for Birns to retire.

In February, Shondor and his attractive girlfriend, fourteen years his junior, were walking downtown when a car with several black men drove by. One of them fired two shots but neither Shondor or his girlfriend were hit. Several months later, Birns walked into an east side bar in response to a meeting requested by several black numbers racketeers. After the downtown drive-by, Shondor must have been expecting more trouble, having decided to bring his heavily armed black bodyguard along. As Birns and his guard entered the bar, they were immediately accosted by several of the numbers men. Eyes glowed hatred as the men shouted curses and threats.

"We want you out of the business or you're dead!" one shouted while pulling back his coat to reveal a pistol in his waistband.

Shondor's bodyguard reacted quickly leveling a small sub-machine gun from under his overcoat. Some customers scurried toward the exits. The group continued shouting at Birns as he and his bodyguard cautiously backed out of the bar and left.

To settle his dispute with Danny Greene, Birns had put up $25,000 with a bookie friend for Greene to be murdered. "And if anything happens to me, make sure they get him," Birns instructed his friend.

Several minor underworld characters, burglars by trade, took on the assignment. On the first attempt, a bomb was planted on Greene's car. But the explosive was wired improperly and it failed to detonate. Greene discovered the bomb when he pulled into a Collinwood service station for gas.

"There's something hanging underneath your car, Mr Greene," the young attendant pointed out.

Danny disassembled the bomb himself, removed the dynamite and brought the rest of the package to Cleveland Police Lt. Edward Kovacic.

Stocky and good-natured, Kovacic grew up in the inner city. He was a career cop who worked just about every existing assignment and eventually retired as police chief. He had known Greene for years, ever since Danny's tenure as president of the International Longshoremen's Association. Back then there had been a group of longshoreman who lived in Kovacic's district and were getting drunk and terrorizing the community. Kovacic went to the I.L.A. headquarters to speak with Greene about the problem.

Danny was just arriving at the office being chauffeured by two longshoremen when Kovacic arrived. One of the dock workers opened the car door and Danny stepped out wearing a men's white fur coat belted at the waist.

"I think we're about to meet Marlon Brando," Ed Kovacic whispered to his partner.

It was the start of a love-hate relationship between Greene and Kovacic.

Not long after that, Greene moved into a house only a block from Kovacic's home. Ed even coached Danny's son in football. Though Kovacic greatly desired to put Danny in the penitentiary, the two men maintained a decent personal relationship. Sometimes their meetings were heated.

"If I tried to approach him with anything he was involved in, it almost always came down to who would throw the first punch," Kovacic recalled. "He would push you as far as you would go. He admired people who had guts, people who stood up to him. If you bent, he would have no use for you."

It was another quality that Celtic warriors exhibited. They admired and respected courage—even that of their enemies. Greene gave the bomb to Kovacic and explained how he found it underneath his car.

"Danny, we can protect you. Let us handle this," Kovacic insisted. "Now where's the dynamite?"

"It's not dynamite Ed, it's C-4.

"Let me have it, Danny."

"I'm going to return it to the old bastard that sent it to me," Greene threatened.

◆　　◆　　◆

During the turn of the century, the area around Christie's Lounge was home to a settlement of Irish immigrants anchored by the celebrated St. Malachi Church. It was a typically cold evening in March of 1975, and the old church was packed at 8:00 P.M. It was Holy Saturday—the night before the most holiest of Catholic holidays—Easter Sunday. The traditional candlelight procession had just begun. It would be an ironic setting for the murder of a Jew by an Irish-Catholic.

Inside Christie's Lounge, Shondor was looking his dapper self, dressed in maroon pants, a white turtleneck shirt and a sport coat. He sipped Henessy with Coke and chatted with friends as go-go dancers flirted overhead. He spoke of retiring and complained about a cold he couldn't shake.

"The warm weather in Miami will help," he said smiling. "Yeah, I think this will be my last month in the rackets."

Birns was happy and relaxed. He finished his drink and said goodbye to the bar owner. A regular patron and friend of Birns accompanied Shondor to the outside of the bar where he said goodbye.

"I'll see you before I leave," Birns promised. A few seconds later, Outside, Shondor reached to unlock the door of his aqua-blue El Dorado.

A St. Malachi parishioner described the explosion as a tremendously loud THUMP or THUD. When the shocked church members ran out to investigate, they were sickened at what they saw, and smelled.

The bomb was definitely overkill—whether intended or not. It was C-4, a potent military explosive. Birns was blown several feet out the roof of the car and landed near the passenger door. The man who walked Birns to his car, braved flames and smoke and located Shondor next to the car. Birns was still alive, though barely. His face, arms and chest were bloodied and blackened. His head and arms convulsed violently as the man reached under Shondor's shoulders to drag him to safety. Birns' body was strangely easy to drag. Peering through the smoke, the man quickly realized why and abandoned his rescue efforts. He only had the upper half of his friend's torso. Birns had been blown in half. His severed legs landed fifty feet away and other parts of him were scattered in various sized, smaller pieces. A chain link fence between Christie's and St. Malachi caught many of the smaller fragments of flesh and bone. At first glance, they resembled steaming pieces of meat.

Though Birns' Cadillac was demolished and smoking heavily, his state-of-the-art burglar alarm survived. The horn was sounding—pulsating faintly as the parking lights flickered dimly. It was an eerie scene with scraps of metal, flesh, glass and clothing scattered about. A dozen tattered and burnt bills—tens, twenties and fifties fluttered along the ground. A leather gym bag and gym shoes had been blown from the trunk. Amazingly, a paper bag of clothing from inside the car survived. It read: "Diamond's of Ohio—Fashions For Men Which Women Love."

Police and bomb squad members worked an entire day examining the devastated scene. Coroner's workers spent hours collecting as many pieces of skin and bone that they could find. A total of $843 in cash was found on or near Birns' body. The Internal Revenue Service promptly claimed the money to be put toward back taxes that Shondor owed.

In weeks to come, investigators headed down the wrong path, concentrating on several black numbers operators as suspects.

"It's dumb to talk about blacks doing Shondor," one said. "Shon wasn't no bad fella. He was white but it didn't make no difference. Shon had a black soul. He was black through and through. Shit, there wasn't no racial prejudice in that goddam Shondor Birns at all. He was a helluva guy. . . No, no, they ain't going to be no more Shondors. . .!"

Shondor's widow was oblivious to the conflict with Danny Greene. Birns had sheltered her from the seamy side of his life. Mourning the dearest and sweetest man she had ever known, and aware that her husband's associate was a pet lover, she gave Shondor's Doberman Pinscher to Danny.

It was a year or so before Greene was blamed for killing Birns. Though Ed Kovacic heard Danny threaten Shondor, he had no direct evidence to build a case. It seemed that everyone knew who did it, but the murder remained officially unsolved. Danny, the proud Catholic, knew his New Testament. "Live by the sword. Die by the sword."

Chapter 20

On a national scale, the mid seventies brought important changes for the country's fight against the powerful Mafia. The federal government acquired several weapons for use against organized crime even though they wouldn't be completely battle-tested until the eighties.

R.I.C.O., or the Racketeer Influenced Corrupt Organization Act, made it possible to penetrate the protective buffer created by the typical mob hierarchy, and convict organized crime bosses based on a pattern of criminal activity. In short, it made it a crime to be a criminal. The sweeping legislation also allowed for the forfeiture of property obtained through illegal profits. Local, state and federal agencies were putting aside territorial disputes and organizing into highly-effective strike forces. Title III of the 1968 Omnibus Crime Control and Safe Streets Act authorized the interception of oral, wire and electronic communications by law enforcement officers investigating serious crimes. Additionally, drug laws had stiffened and WITSEC, the F.B.I.'s witness protection program, was becoming an attractive alternative to prison time for those criminals with valuable knowledge.

The Mafia had remained protected from such espionage due to its enforcement of omerta. But La Cosa Nostra was going through its own changes. The secret society was aging and the new members coming in were not the street toughened criminals that their fathers and uncles had been.

Chapter 21

In 1974, Danny Greene left his faithful and long-suffering wife Nancy and their two daughters, and rented an apartment on Waterloo Road—a fitting street name for a man at war. Making Greene feel at home was a short side street called Daniel, just a block away. And E. 147th Street, where he spent much of his childhood, was right around the corner. Only seconds from access to Interstate 90, Waterloo was a short, commercial strip of bars, mom-and-pop businesses, ethnic food stores, gas stations and small apartment buildings.

Danny's new home was a two-story brick building with a store-front on the bottom and a large apartment on top. He rented a small house in the rear of the property and often had business meetings there. One of the first things Danny did when he moved in was spray a flourishing grape vine with vegetation killer because it blocked his view from a window.

In the dining room which had mirrored walls, he set up a weight bench. In his forties now, Greene was becoming very conscious of his health and appearance even to the point of having painful transplants to hide his hair loss. He lifted weights and jogged daily. For a while, Danny was on a diet consisting mainly of fish, seeds and vitamins. He frequented a Collinwood fruit market favoring their apple cider and fancied Chinese food. Often when at a restaurant, Danny ordered only a cup of hot water, supplying his own tea bag. Still, he'd leave a generous tip.

Inside a closet at his apartment, Greene kept a small arsenal—rifles, handguns and numerous boxes of ammo, even hand grenades. Danny had a fondness for telephones. He had five installed in the relatively small apartment that he rented. In these days before designer phones, Danny had a friend take all of the phones to receive a special plating, making them green.

Outside, Danny made a habit of putting out food for the birds and squirrels. He had always been an animal lover and owned two cats.

Greene became known quickly on Waterloo. Those who didn't know him were sure to find out who he was, perhaps when Danny was driving by in his green Lincoln, or when he was sitting on a lawn chair outside his apartment while basking in the sun.

"Do you know who that is?

"No."

"Why that's Danny Greene," was a frequent exchange for months while Danny was a new-comer to Waterloo. Greene made sure the neighborhood undesirables knew who was in charge. He kicked out a bookmaker who operated out of a small Waterloo business and kept a local bar in line with personal visits, if things got too loud or disorderly. When a rowdy group of Hell's Angels thundered into town, Greene visited their headquarters with a stick of dynamite. He threatened to light it and throw it into their club house until they came out to receive a warning to keep things quiet when in Collinwood.

Two doors down from Danny was an old barber that he began patronizing. Greene became fond of the barber despite his Italian ancestry.

"I hate those fucking dagos," Danny once told the man. "You're the only one I like. If they get me with a machine gun while I'm in your barber's chair, you'll probably be going with me," Danny joked. "But seriously, if anyone ever bothers you, you make sure you come and tell me."

On Waterloo, Danny became a favorite with neighborhood children whom he paid five, even ten dollars for running a quick errand. The parking lot next to Greene's building was favorite for kids to roller skate. Danny used to open his window, and throw out a handful of change for them to skate by and scoop up. He made frequent cash donations to needy neighbors and if he knew ahead of time that one was stopping at the butcher shop several doors down, he would phone ahead.

"A friend will be down this afternoon," he might tell the butcher. Give her what she wants and I'll be down later to take care of it."

"You got it Danny."

Every Thanksgiving and Christmas, Danny bought fifty, twenty-pound turkeys and with the help of friends, passed them out to his neighbors. If he saw a friend, neighbor or acquaintance at a restaurant, Danny often picked up the tab. The waitresses loved him for his generous tips. So did the red-headed Irish-American, teenage girl who delivered Danny's newspaper. She could be assured of a $5.00 payment even though Danny's bill was less than $2.50. Eventually Danny took such a liking to the girl that he paid her way through Villa Angela Academy, a private Catholic girls' school in Collinwood. For another neighborhood girl, Danny paid for braces.

Danny Greene might have been a racketeer, but he had a deep desire, a need to be liked in the "square world" as he would call it. But his goodwill was not graciously received by all. One afternoon Danny drove to a church in a poor neighborhood to make a rather unconventional donation to a nun he had known from grade school. He knocked on the door of the convent and the sister answered.

"No Danny, I cannot accept that," the nun insisted.

"I'll just leave it on the steps sister. You don't even have to know where it came from."

"Thank you Danny but no," she said firmly while closing the door.

What the nun was refusing to accept was a whole bucket full of loose coins.

Back on Waterloo, Danny had succeeded at becoming a beloved neighborhood celebrity, despite his line of work. By this time, he was trying to make a name for himself in the fire clean-up and repair industry. Often referred to as firechasers, the businesses monitor fire department radio calls and speed to the scenes of burned-out buildings to propose their services to property owners. One company was emerging as supreme, using high-pressure sales tactics and threats to competitors. Bombings, fires and other violence were becoming commonplace. Greene tried to enter the scene as a peacemaker. It would be a racket not unlike the set-up that Shondor Birns had with the black numbers operators. For a couple thousand dollars, Danny would give a firechasing firm a guarantee against interference from competitors.

But Greene's nemesis, Ed Kovacic and other Cleveland Police Intelligence investigators were again onto him. Since Greene's days as president of the longshoremen's union, Kovacic had been hounding him. He followed Danny around, pestered, and questioned him often, and kept abreast of his affairs. But their relationship wasn't all bad.

When Greene was falsely accused of the shooting of a black city official, Kovacic reassured him.

"Danny I don't think you did it. And I would never send you away for something you didn't do."

After hearing that, Greene had the utmost respect for Kovacic. Greene's implication in the attempted murder ended up being a case of mistaken identity.

Kovacic was convinced that he could learn much about organized crime from Greene. The F.B.I. was one step ahead though, and had cultivated Danny into a top-echelon informant. Like Teamster boss Jackie Presser, Danny played the dangerous informant game, believing the benefits outweighed the risks. He even gave himself a code name— Mr. Patrick. It was both the name he was confirmed with as a child and that of his beloved Irish saint. Danny insisted that the F.B.I. use the monicker when contacting him.

Before Danny could establish a foothold in the firechasing racket, his plans folded under the pressure of Kovacic nosing around. Greene denied any involvement.

"I don't get a dime, no one has offered me a dime and I don't want a dime from any of them. That industry might need straightening out, I don't know. But I don't want in it."

Chapter 22

Ed Kovacic was up early enjoying breakfast when he heard two explosions off in the distance.

"Danny Greene was just killed," Kovacic predicted to his wife.

At Greene's apartment, one bomb was thrown through a kitchen window. A second bomb, several times more powerful then the first, awaited Greene at the back of the building should he somehow survive the first blast.

Danny had already awakened to the sound of the window shattering and was on his feet immediately with a .38 revolver in hand. He started heading for the bedroom door when the first bomb exploded, blowing out one side of the building and demolishing the kitchen. A portion of the bedroom floor that Greene was standing on caved in. Danny was sent tumbling down to the kitchen. He fell next to the refrigerator which had tipped to one side, trapping him in a protective cove. As luck would have it, Greene was shielded from lethal chunks of brick, plaster and wood and shards of widow glass and dishes.

Danny's two dogs escaped from the rubble, but two of his four cats did not fare as well. They were asleep in the kitchen and awakened to the sound of the bomb being thrown through the window. Dashing over to investigate the strange object, the animals were killed instantly when it exploded.

Danny rose quickly, having suffered only a broken rib. He headed for Debbie, his teenage mistress, up in the bedroom. She had also narrowly escaped death as an air conditioner was blown from the window landing inches from her head. Leading his stunned girlfriend with one hand and holding his other hand to his chest, Danny confidently picked his way through the rubble, pieces of his dead pets and numerous $50 and $100 bills. They made it safely outside to Greene's Lincoln and left the area.

When police and the bomb squad arrived on the scene they found the unexploded bomb at the rear of the demolished building. The package consisted of a large chunk of C2 military plastic explosive strapped to a five gallon can of gasoline.

Later bomb experts discovered that the blasting caps were faulty. Witnesses reported hearing what sounded like two gunshots moments after the two bombs exploded. Those were the blasting caps. The problem was that they were not large enough to detonate the C2. A bomb technician commented that if this bomb had gone off, half of the block would have gone up in flames. Lucky for Collinwood. And lucky for Danny Greene. It was at least the fourth murder attempt on the Irishman. Like the infinitely swirling pattern of knotwork, the Celtic art form, there seemed to be no end to the life of Danny Greene.

Two days after the Waterloo bombing, the rubble was cleared away leaving an empty lot. The next day the Celtic warrior was back. Nobody was going to force Danny Greene from his turf. Immediately Danny had two trailers set up in the empty lot. One would be his residence and the other would serve as an office.

Now it was war. Danny organized the toughest of his young followers into the Celtic Club, a small organization set up like a corporation but described more appropriately as the Irish Mafia. He had a sign erected outside his trailers declaring the area, "Future Home of the Celtic Club." A green harp, a traditional Celtic symbol, adorned the sign and nearby, fluttering in the lake breezes, was the Irish Tri-Color. Beneath the flag, Danny Greene sat bare-chested on a lawn chair or wooden bench as his Celtic soldiers eyed passing cars. Not since the Prohibition-era days of Chicago's florist shop owner and racketeer Dion O'Banion, had there been such a powerful and colorful Irish-American gangster.

Among Danny's top Celtic Club representatives were Keith Ritson, Kevin McTaggart and Brian O'Donnell.

Ritson was a burly, 28-year-old with bushy hair. A roofer by trade, he had arrests for burglary, carrying a concealed weapon and possession of criminal tools.

Tall and blonde, 19-year-old McTaggart called Greene his uncle.

He was a stagehand at the Cleveland Convention Center and a lighting man at the Roxy Bar and Grille on Short Vincent Avenue. McTaggart also served as a liaison to the Hell's Angels, who were occasionally hired by Danny as muscle.

Brian O'Donnell, a bar owner, was the brightest of the crew and served as financial director. He helped Danny pass out Celtic cross pendants direct from Ireland. Youngest in the group was Greene's own teenage son, Danny Jr., who often accompanied his dad on business errands, and guarded his car. Greene's old friend, Billy McDuffy, frequently served in the same capacity. Other Celtic Club henchmen included an Irish-American ex-Cleveland police officer, and even a black, county jail official.

Greene dubbed his men with the names of famous Celtic warriors and even quizzed them on Irish history. He supplied them with green business cards and green ink pens to pass out. He kept in contact with them via modern belt pagers, a fairly new addition to communication technology.

Danny also had numerous associates of the Celtic Club. Elmer Brittain ran high-stakes card games on the west side of town. Ernest "Ted" Waite met Danny Greene from working in the fire chasing business.

After organizing the Celtic Club, Danny played up the failed Waterloo Avenue bombing to the hilt, flaunting his growing legend of invincibility. For a newspaper photographer, he posed proudly in front of a boarded-up window of his obliterated apartment building. He granted interviews to all the television stations in town.

"The luck of the Irish is with me," he boldly declared to one television reporter. "And I have a message for those yellow maggots. That includes the payers and the doers. The doers are the people who carried out the bombing. They have to be eliminated because the people who paid them can't afford to have them remain alive. And the payers are going to feel great heat from the F.B.I. and the local authorities. . . And let me clear something else up. I didn't run away from the explosion. Someone said they saw me running away. I walked away."

The reporter suggested to Danny that he had nine lives.

"I'm an Irish-Catholic," Danny responded. "I believe that the Guy Upstairs pulls the strings, and you're not going to go until He says so. It just wasn't my time yet."

"Danny is a fatalist," said a good friend of his. "He told me he fig-ure's he's going to get it some day. But it doesn't seem to bother him. He's says he's going to try to make all the money he can while he's still around."

After the bombing, John Nardi approached Danny Greene. Nardi was hoping to claim a piece of the rackets for himself but lacked the necessary muscle.

"Your enemies are my enemies," Nardi told Greene. "Let's fight them together."

Danny agreed. Though he harbored ill feelings toward many Italians, Greene cooperated with them whenever it was in his best interest.

After Danny's bold challenge appeared on television, a young Greene wannabee was so impressed with his hero, that he honored the Irishman with the following poem. It is entitled The Ballad of Danny Greene.

> *Among the Crow, the story says,*
> *A man was judged by fiercest foe.*
> *Many scalps a brave Chief took,*
> *Who fought his way to fame,*
> *Often he outwitted death,*
> *Ere history prized his name.*
> *A modern warrior known as Greene*
> *Was very quick and smart, and mean.*
> *He scrambled hard and fought like hell,*
> *And led a charmed existence.*
> *They shot him down and blew him up*
> *With most regular persistence.*
> *Through guile and luck and skill,*
> *Danny Greene is with us still.*
> *He does his job as he must do,*
> *With zeal, finesse and pride.*
> *It's hard to keep a good man down,*
> *With Saint Patrick at his side.*
> *Some day he'll die, as all we must,*
> *Some will laugh but most will cry.*

His legend will live on for years,
To bring his friends mixed pleasure,
For he has done both bad and good,
And lived his life full measure.

Danny couldn't have been more proud.

Ed Kovacic wanted to put Greene under police protection, but Danny refused.

"They're gonna kill you Danny, you know that don't you?"

"Well Ed, if they ever do get me, it's going to be with a bomb. But then again, there's not a bomb big enough to kill Danny Greene."

With his confidence peaking, Danny continued to taunt his would-be executioners. Sometimes he was cautious—sometimes he was downright foolhardy. In the evening before he retired, he placed a pebble on the hood of his green Lincoln. In the morning he checked to make sure the pebble was in place, then got on his hands and knees to check under the vehicle. In the late evening hours, Greene stood in the window of his lighted bedroom making himself an easy target. During the night, he sometimes sat in a chair on the roof of the next building surveilling his turf for signs of intruders. At his feet was a high-powered rifle.

The police set up their own undercover detail to protect Greene. For several weeks they guarded his property from an unmarked van. Being the vainglorious host he was, Danny once flustered the detectives by having several sandwiches and soft drinks delivered to the unmarked police van.

"Danny, we're here to protect you. You're gonna blow our cover," one officer scolded.

"Well it was close to lunch time. I though you guys might be hungry," Greene reasoned.

◆　　　◆　　　◆

Across the street from Greene's trailer lived a mother of six children. Her husband had recently left her. Greene admired the woman, an Irish-American named Patty, for holding her head high and not complaining despite her hardships. Danny introduced himself one day and the two chatted.

"Do you know what I do?" he asked her.

"I don't care what you do. What you do is your business," she answered.

"I know you're an honest person because you look me straight in the eye. I like that. And I like the fact that you're Irish."

"Irish people can be cold sometimes though," Patty offered.

"I can be cold when I want to be," Danny replied.

Knowing that Patty was facing the loss of her home, Danny offered his house in the rear for her and her children.

"I'd consider it a favor if you moved in. You could keep an eye on things. You know, keep it private for me."

Patty agreed and took up residence in Greene's house. Danny parked his car under Patty's kitchen window. Patty had a dog that always barked when someone walked by. But Danny didn't mind. He even encouraged her to keep the dog outside.

"You should have lived here before my building was blown up."

The two took a liking to each other and had frequent heart-to-heart chats. A bold and candid person, Patty often talked to Danny about the path he had chosen in life.

"I knew when I was fourteen I didn't want a regular job. I wanted excitement and wanted people to know who I was, to respect me. But I also want them to know that I have a good side despite what I do."

Patty even rebuked Greene for the danger he lived with.

"How can you go through life always having to look over your shoulder?"

"Hey I'm Irish Catholic. I've got the best guardian angel there is," Danny replied. "Besides the man upstairs pulls the strings. I'm not going anywhere until he says so."

"Do you think you're going to get to heaven because of all the money that you give away," Patty asked candidly.

Danny laughed and shook his head.

"Boy the things you come up with," he said. "That's what I like about you. Now don't you know that all us Irish people all go to heaven?"

Chapter 23

In 1975, Danny Greene attempted to establish himself in the vending machine racket. which had often been a Mafia-dominated business. Cigarette machines, candy machines, coin-operated washers and dryers all bring easy profits, especially if competition is limited.

Thomas J. Sinito was a Mafia lieutenant under Angelo "Big Ange" Lonardo. His involvement with Lonardo began when he worked as a bartender at Angelo's Highlander Restaurant and Lounge. Later, Sinito had several of his own ventures, including part ownership in a Valley Forge, Pennsylvania amusement park. Locally, Sinito entered the vending business with lucrative washer and dryer accounts at numerous apartment buildings. Sinito's front was a gift basket company, on Chagrin Boulevard, once a favored area for Mafia business and socialization.

According to a mob informant, Tommy Sinito was drawn into the conflict with Danny.

"Sinito felt that Greene was trying to extort every motel and apartment that he had washers and dryers. . . Tommy found a bomb on his car attached to the frame and destroyed it."

Other vending machine dealers competing with Greene weren't so lucky.

Officers were dispatched to the Days Inn at Route 46 and Interstate 80, Austintown Township, Ohio. This officer found the body of a white male bound and gagged with tape lying face down in a small pool of water about eight inches deep under an oak tree. The unknown male was wearing a gray tweed suit with a blue short sleeve shirt. The unknown male's pants were pulled below his knees and all his pockets were out. The unknown male was wearing blue socks, one black 10 1/2 low cut shoe, and the black right shoe 10 1/2 was on the ground about 30' southwest of the body. The unknown male was wearing a gold wedding band on his left hand. The victim appeared to be 40-50 years old; 5'9" tall; weighing 180 pounds; black hair mixed with gray. The crime scene was roped off and the County Coroner was notified.

The unknown male referred to in the homicide report was later identified as John Conte. Conte had his own vending business, and was also a route man for another company that provided slot machines for parties and private clubs. Conte was also a friend of Joseph C. Gallo, a known mob figure, and later, a partner of Sinito. Gallo was indicted but acquitted for the bombing of Danny Greene's apartment. (Moe Kiraly, a Mafia associate, was convicted in the case and sent to prison.)

On the day of his murder, Conte told his wife he was going to meet with Danny Greene. Police theorized that Conte was beaten to death in Danny's trailer and the body transported to Austintown Township, in Ohio's Mahoning Valley. They conducted a search of the trailer and confiscated a baseball bat, lengths of phone wire, electrical cord and floor tiles which had buckled from excessive moisture—possibly soapy water used to remove blood stains. The evidence was sent to a crime lab for analysis. Danny was never officially implicated in the killing of Conte, which was reportedly ordered by John Nardi.

P A R T 3

Mafia War

Primary Characters

- Ronald "Ronnie Crab" Carabbia: *Mafia lieutenant from Mahoning Valley*
- Eugene "the Animal" Ciasullo: *Mafia enforcer*
- Butchie Cisternino: *Mafia soldier*
- Ray Ferritto: *Mafia soldier*
- Jimmy "the Weasel" Fratianno: *California mob captain*
- Danny Greene: *Irish-American racketeer*
- James "Jack White" Licavoli: *Mafia boss*
- Angelo "Big Ange" Lonardo: *Mafia underboss*
- Leo "Lips" Moceri: *Mafia underboss*
- John Nardi: *Union official; Mafia associate*

Chapter 24

John Scalish was Cleveland's handsome, silver-haired Mafia don of three decades. A suave, quiet man, he spent much of his leisure time on the waters of Lake Erie entertaining prominent citizens in his impressive yacht. Scalish was not one to pursue new schemes. He was content living well off the profits from Las Vegas skim—money stolen from casino profits before being counted for taxes. For years, Scalish ran Buckeye Vending Company, known for its strong-arm tactics. His partners in Buckeye were senior mob members Frank Embrescia and Milton "Maishe" Rockman .

Milton "Maishe" Rockman was the mob's unofficial treasurer and link to the Teamster's union via his friendship with union president Jackie Presser. Also called "Deer Hunter" because of his love of big game hunting, Rockman was described as a low-key, quiet figure who preferred to stay at home rather than frequent the usual mob hangouts. He was never associated with any of the gang violence connected to the Scalish Mafia family.

"He was hands off with the heavy-handed stuff," a federal investigator commented.

Born a Jew, Rockman became a constant companion of Scalish and later converted to Catholicism, taking communion twice a week. He even wound up marrying one of Scalish's sisters. Maishe was so close with John Scalish that he would have been officially inducted into the mob if he had some Italian blood. Official membership notwithstanding, Rockman commanded as much respect and power as any Mafia underboss.

Mafia lieutenant Angelo Lonardo, also married a sister of John Scalish. The three couples even lived in the same area of Pepper Pike, an affluent suburb on Cleveland's east side. Teamster official and mob associate Babe Triscaro also lived in the area. The F.B.I. conducted so much surveillance in the small neighborhood, they dubbed it "the compound."

Scalish had been plagued by heart problems and cancer for several years. In May of 1976, he went in for delicate bypass surgery. Scalish made it through the operation, but succumbed several hours later in the recovery room. News of his death swept through the underworld.

His funeral was reminiscent of the extravagant send-offs given the Lonardo and Porrello brothers during Prohibition. Scalish's body was laid to rest in a gold inlaid casket and the solemn mass was said by three priests. Miles of black Cadillacs and Lincolns followed the hearse to Calvary Cemetery.

Although Scalish did not announce his choice of a successor, Rockman reported that during his last days, Scalish personally informed him that he wanted Jack Licavoli to replace him. At the time, Licavoli was one of the older, more respected members of the Cleveland family and was once underboss of the Youngstown rackets.

Rockman's announcement came as a surprise to many, including Licavoli, who wanted nothing to do with running the Cleveland rackets. Lonardo was considered by most to be the logical replacement for Scalish. He had more contacts with other mob families and was more familiar with Mafia business formalities. In earlier years, even Al Polizzi, who preceded Scalish as Cleveland don, had recommended that Lonardo be next in line. Even Licavoli himself knew he was short on knowledge of Mafia protocol.

"Angelo speaks better English and has more contacts," he complained.

"Take it Jack, that's what Johnny wanted," Lonardo said.

Licavoli was an unlikely choice for Mafia chieftain. Although he had amassed a fortune from gambling enterprises, he was little more than a stingy old man, satisfied living as a bachelor in his tiny Little Italy house with the strings of garlic hanging outside the back door. Since his income had never been declared, he was even able to draw a monthly Social Security check.

Lonardo didn't say anything, but he suspected Rockman of lying about Scalish's choice of successor. Perhaps Rockman felt he could influence Licavoli's decisions easier than Lonardo's.

Reluctantly, the 72-year-old former Detroit Purple Gang member assumed leadership. Up until then, Licavoli had been content playing golf and making homemade wine. By then he was more often referred to as Jack White or "Blackie" both plays on his dark complexion.

By 1970, James Licavoli had become known as the "king of the hill"—Murray Hill in Little Italy. He lived with a roommate, another seventy-year-old bachelor, who worked as a carpenter. Their home was furnished with a statue of the Virgin Mary around which a Holy Rosary was draped. Over the statue hung a provocative oil painting of a sexy woman undressing. In another room, Licavoli had a custom-made whirlpool and steam bath to nurse his arthritic knees. In a dresser drawer, beneath his underwear, he kept several thousand dollars in cash.

Licavoli could often be found passing the hours on a Mayfield Road bench outside the card shop or the Roman Gardens restaurant, a short walk from his house. There the short, stout and aging Mafioso chatted with friends and mob wannabees while he leaned on his treasured wooden cane, a prized possession which concealed a glistening, razor-sharp blade.

Despite Licavoli's great wealth, he was known for being cheap and occasionally foolish—to the point of embarrassment. Once at a local mall, he was detained by store detectives for switching the price tags on a pair of pants. After hearing about the background of their shoplifter, the department store manager shuddered and declined to prosecute. Another time, Licavoli was caught putting slugs in a vending machine and he also used stolen credit cards on vacations.

In Little Italy, Licavoli had control of one of the most lucrative barbut games in the region. He received a weekly profit from the fast-paced Greek dice game which was run by Butchie Cisternino. Cisternino was a tough, blue-eyed, good-looking mob associate and devoted father of five.

The barbut games were held in several Little Italy locations including the card shop, a mob hangout, and another spot known as "the library." Licavoli attended the games frequently and was treated like a god. On occasion, he boosted attendance by helping to prepare the food served there. Another popular mob-run gambling spot was the Pineway Trails Sportsmans Club. Located in a rural northeast

Ohio area, it ran for only a year before being closed down by law enforcement.

As his consigliere, or counselor, Licavoli named Tony Delsanter and appointed his cousin Leo Moceri as underboss. Moceri had been running the rackets in Akron, fifty miles south of Cleveland.

Christened Calogero Moceri in 1907, Leo was a muscular and active man still feared and respected nationally as a senior La Cosa Nostra member. He had been described as a "deadpan character with cold eyes who speaks tersely through heavy lips."

"When you talk to Moceri, you get a cordial reply as to his name and address plus an icy stare—nothing more," a police official once commented.

At age sixty-nine, Leo Moceri was in good health except for recent gall bladder surgery and poor fitting dentures which he had been complaining about. He had a long history of arrests, including three murder indictments from Toledo. One was for the death of an Ohio beer baron. Moceri escaped prosecution on all three. Perhaps his use of sixteen aliases helped. In 1969, he was acquitted of income tax evasion. Incredibly, he claimed that he had no income but instead was living on the profits from his days as a bootlegger. Though finances were never a problem for Leo, he was once caught putting slugs in a pay phone to make a long distance call.

Moceri had a friend who owned a successful fruit market. Once he told the man, "If I knew I could make that much money selling fruit, I would have never killed all those people." It was a sad commentary on a misspent life.

Leo had been single since he was divorced from his first wife in 1961 in Florida. In Ohio, he settled in an exclusive suburb north of Akron, in a stately English-style stone home, with a huge wooded lot set back 1000 feet from the roadway. He didn't carry a gun, nor did he have one in his house. He didn't need one. Anybody who knew what was good for him would never mess with Lips.

Moceri did have a girlfriend, but he was a loaner who sometimes suddenly left town in his Mercedes for short business trips. He and his girlfriend hoped to retire to a farm outside of Akron. He spent much of his time in Warren and could often be found out on a golf course or dining at Cherry's Restaurant where many of the Pennsylvania and Ohio Mafiosi met.

Moceri kept quite busy loansharking and with various other rackets. He had numerous business interests including real estate. He was a partner in an Akron bingo hall and received a cut of the gambling profits at the popular Little Italy Feast of the Assumption.

It was at this feast that Moceri and John Nardi, longtime enemies had a bitter argument. Nardi demanded that he should receive a cut of the festival's gambling profits.

"You'll get nothing!" Moceri yelled. "You keep your hands off the rackets and get rid of that Irish bastard."

"I'll do what I want to do!" Nardi countered.

"Do you know who I am!" Moceri screamed. "I'm Leo Moceri and nobody pushes me around!"

After hearing of the argument, Licavoli was quite disturbed. He wanted Nardi and his cousin to make peace but Tony Delsanter encouraged him to have both Nardi and Greene murdered. Licavoli waited. Nardi didn't.

Chapter 25

By 1975, John Nardi's gambling habit was taking a toll. He was heavily in debt to several bookmakers, and Caesars Palace in Las Vegas was suing him over a $10,000 casino tab.

Through his connection to mob associate Dominick Bartone, Nardi fell into a drug smuggling scheme he thought might solve his financial problems. In 1959, Bartone was convicted in Miami for bribing customs agents and conspiring to ship arms and planes to Anti-Castro forces in the Dominican Republic. Another interesting partner in the drug deal was Mitch WerBell, an international arms dealer from Georgia. Reportedly, WerBell once worked for the C.I.A. Morton Franklin was the last principal. He was an insurance man and along with Bartone was implicated in the bankruptcy case of an Ohio bank.

Before the smuggling plan was executed, Florida investigators were on the move with indictments. Apparently they had a confidential informant.

Report of Air Crash

Investigation disclosed the decedent expired as the result of injuries sustained in an air crash which occurred in the Mojave desert at a location approximately 2 miles East of the Mojave Airport and approximately 1 mile north of State Route 58, Mojave, Rural, California. . . The events prior to the air crash would indicate the decedent was piloting a F-51-D Mustang. . . The decedent was flying Northbound toward the Mojave airport at about 5,000 feet. He indicated by radio that he was going down and run the pylons and implemented a slow down-

ward roll. During the roll, he made the statement, "Oh, oh, no!", and apparently applied power in an effort to pull out of the roll, however, he did not have enough altitude to recover and impacted the ground.

The decedent referred to in the report was Kenneth Burnstine, 43, of Fort Lauderdale, Florida. Burnstine was the pilot for the drug smuggling operation. As it turned out, Burnstine was the informant working with investigators. Despite the obvious suspicion, none of the Bartone smuggling ring members were officially connected with their pilot's sudden death.

Chapter 26

In his eighties, Tony Milano was a dignified, but lonely man, who had lost most of his close friends to the average life expectancy. He had grayish-white hair, wore thick glasses and was hard of hearing. A chain smoker of Lucky Strikes, Milano attributed his longevity to a diet high in fruits and vegetables. He never drank water and professed to be his own doctor. Milano could often be found taking a casual walk in Little Italy where he passed out candy to neighborhood kids.

His office was smoke-filled and lined with bookcases. On a wall hung a picture of Abraham Lincoln. Next to that was a framed photograph of President Richard Nixon signed, "To Anthony Milano—with best wishes." On his desk he kept a thermos of hot espresso that he brought fresh from home daily. Guests were served from white demitasse cups.

Milano was not one to grant interviews, but on occasion he spoke with Cleveland Press reporter Tony Natale, or Mairy Jayn Woge of the Plain Dealer. Naturally, they took the opportunity to ask about the "M" word. But Milano adamantly denied its existence.

"Mafia! Mafia! That's all I hear! The newspapers. The police. There is no such thing as the Mafia. Years ago when Italy was divided into states and rich barons ruled, there was a Mafia. It was started by bandits who stole from the rich. There is no such thing. Valachi? Baloney. He just told the government what it wanted to hear. And if the F.B.I. knows so much about it, why don't they get somebody into it. The only thing they're concerned about is the black list of Italians they want killed."

(Ironically, when Milano made that statement, a top-secret plan was being readied by the F.B.I. to place a young undercover agent in

the midst of the Bonnano Mafia family in New York. It was a phe-
nomenally successful six-year operation.)

In Tony Milano's last years he spent his time playing chess and
recording his words of his wisdom in a pamphlet he titled
"Philosophical Quotations by Anthony Milano."

A sampling:

*Grace, courtesy and elegance are the arts that contribute to
make life more pleasurable and beautiful.*
He who thinks he is so great, suddenly falls.
*Do everything you can, don't spend all you have, don't believe
everything you hear and don't tell everything you know.*
*In order to become dominator, it is necessary to give the people
discipline, education, liberty and bread.*
If you want to live in peace, look, listen and be quiet.
Study first the penal code, and then go swimming.
The secret of power is desire.

Chapter 27

Eugene Ciasullo was an independent mob enforcer with connections to Mafia bosses in several cities. He was greatly feared as the brightest and most capable of Cleveland mob figures loyal to John Scalish and Jack Licavoli.

Born in 1931, Ciasullo was raised on the tough streets of East Cleveland, a changing community with more crime per capita than Cleveland proper. Though only 5' 8" tall, Eugene was burly, muscular and mean, and thus an effective member of the Shaw High School Football team.

In years to come, Eugene decided that the streets offered more money and excitement than the lathing and plastering trades he learned from his uncles. His entry in the underworld was via thefts and burglaries with men like Butchie Cisternino with whom Eugene became very close. Later the two got into the loan business "renting" money for 5% weekly. If the loan amount was $1,000, then the borrower had to pay $50 in vigoorish or interest weekly, until the entire principal was repaid. Cisternino's and Ciasullo's system of renting money would be copied by loansharks across the country.

Eugene Ciasullo was notorious for his hair trigger temper. Though his gap-toothed face could be lit brightly with laughter, anger him, and there was a very dark side, a natural ferocity that instantly emerged accentuated by intimidating, shark-like eyes. It could simply be someone interfering in an argument between Eugene and a girlfriend, insulting a friend or cutting him off on the road. The result was another statistic—a bloodied and or battered victim of Eugene's rage, his meaty hands or maybe a nearby weapon like the old bladed lathing hatchet he kept under his car seat. On one occasion it was, of all things, a cue ball that Ciasullo used to inflict numerous skull fractures during a bar fight. It was that particularly brutal attack that prompted an F.B.I. agent to dub Ciasullo, "the Animal."

There were those who had to brag that they were tough and mean to satisfy their own insecurities. Then there was Eugene Ciasullo. He was quiet in that respect but his reputation preceded him. Thus Ciasullo attracted the attention of high-ranking La Cosa Nostra members. He quickly became a busy and effective Mafia enforcer. On occasion requests came in to John Scalish for the Animal to take care of a "headache" for another mob family.

In the late sixties, Ciasullo worked as a collector for King's Castle Casino in Lake Tahoe. Before the convenience of automated teller machines, high-rolling gamblers could often get cash advances from the casino. However the money was not a legal loan according to state law, so if a player skipped town owing a significant amount, the casino had little recourse. Pursuit of civil action in other states was legally complicated and cost prohibitive. That's where men like Eugene Ciasullo came in.

The job took him across the nation to the front doors of Nevada gamblers who skipped out on their cash advance tabs. They were met at the front door by Eugene and perhaps a baseball bat. When not on the road collecting, Eugene often spent time in Lake Tahoe with well-known bookie and professional gambler Joe "The Hat" Lanese. On occasion, even Eugene's name could be found lingering on the debtor's list for King's Castle. Once the Casino manager complained to Joe Lanese.

"You know Eugene owes us a lot of money, Joe."

"Listen," Lanese replied. "Fill up a barrel with chips and let him play."

"What?"

"That's right," Lanese said. "Fill up a barrel with chips and let him play cause Eugene ain't gonna win. He ain't gonna win. And if he wins, let him play some more cause he'll lose it right back."

Such was Ciasullo's gambling life. Consistently luckless. He was a bad better and a worse loser. Some collector's had their lists "checked" by persons familiar with the gaming industry and its underworld influences. "Don't go there," they'd usually advise while pointing to the Animal's name and home address. Eugene found it difficult to resist the lure of the green felt and though his name turned up on the collection lists of other casinos, none of their representatives ever showed up at his door. With this privilege, Ciasullo's reputation continued to grow.

Eugene enjoyed the fast-paced world of entertainment found in Nevada. When not losing money at a table, he could be found spending it on drinks for cohorts, influential contacts and women, by whom Eugene was well admired for his old-fashioned class. He was the first at the table to rise for a lady seated near him and the quickest to light her cigarette.

Among the many stars Ciasullo met, Sammy Davis Jr. was his favorite. He became acquainted with "Mr. Entertainment" after Davis opened the Front Row Theater, Cleveland's former premier theater-in-the-round once owned by Jackie Presser. Backstage, in luxurious suites or top restaurants, Eugene could occasionally be found yucking it up at lavish parties given by Sammy.

That was typical of Eugene's social life. But business life was nothing to laugh at. By the time John Scalish died in 1976, Eugene the Animal was suspected of numerous mob murders and vicious assaults across the country. But not once was evidence uncovered to indict, let alone convict him. By the seventies, he and Butchie Cisternino emerged as the leaders of a group of young Collinwood thieves and burglars who were dubbed the "Young Turks," by the local media. These men, who included Joe "Loose" Iacobacci, Alfred "Allie" Calabrese and Joe Bonariggo, became the frontline soldiers in the Cleveland mob's war with Danny Greene and John Nardi.

Chapter 28

It was 1:00 o'clock in the morning on July 21, 1976, and there was no warning. Eugene Ciasullo had just exited his Lincoln Mark IV and was walking up his front porch steps. When he reached the top, a small bomb, concealed in a flower pot in front of the door, exploded. Eugene was struck in the stomach with dozens of concrete nails which had been packed in the flower pot to act as shrapnel. The blast slammed Ciasullo into his front door which collapsed in. He struggled to his feet, but didn't enter his house for fear of jeopardizing his family's security. Instead, Eugene pulled a .38-caliber revolver from his waistband and ducked into the darkness of his backyard. His would-be-assassin might move in to finish him off. Though critically wounded, Ciasullo hoped to be waiting.

By then, the two bombers, rumored to be a Greene associate and a member of the Hell's Angels, were almost to their car which was parked on the opposite side of wooded area across from Ciasullo's home. With one arm tucked firmly in his side, Eugene hopped numerous fences, making his way to the home of an uncle. He banged on the door and within a few minutes, an ambulance was racing Ciasullo to a nearby hospital.

Word of the bombing spread quickly through the ranks of the Cleveland Mafia. Butchie Cisternino and his crew were devastated. If Greene could do this to Eugene, then they were all in grave danger.

At the hospital, x-rays showed that dozens of the nails had ripped into Eugene's intestines, stomach and gall bladder. He wasn't expected to last the night but still Butchie Cisternino and Ciasullo's lifelong friend Jimmy Martino stood guard outside his room, declining an offer of police protection.

Amazingly, Eugene's condition improved. For two weeks his mother came daily to sit at his bedside. There she knit and prayed for her son. Though Cisternino or Martino were always outside the door working in shifts to guard Ciasullo, Eugene kept a revolver stashed in his mother's knitting bag.

Eugene had surgery in which his gall bladder and part of his intestines were removed. His condition improved but it would be slow going. After two weeks in the hospital, he flew to Florida and took up residence at his home there to recuperate.

After a few weeks, Cisternino begged Ciasullo to return and rejoin the war against Danny Greene. Eugene was upset that Butchie asked him to return after he had almost been killed.

"You guys kill someone yourselves, then I'll come back, " Eugene demanded.

Chapter 29

The Mafia's war with Danny Greene hits its peak in 1976. In August, only weeks after mob enforcer Eugene Ciasullo was bombed, feared underboss Leo Moceri received a threatening phone call.

"Leo you're dead," the unidentified caller said.

His girlfriend expressed concern over the call, but Leo laughed.

"If anyone wanted to kill me I wouldn't get a call about it," he told her. "They would just do it."

Two weeks after the phone call, Moceri disappeared. Several days later his Mercedes was found abandoned. In the trunk were a set of golf clubs that Leo had won. They were laying in a pool of blood infested with maggot larvae. Moceri's body was never found.

Other violence followed as Danny Greene sent out members of his Celtic Club to eliminate potential competition in the rackets, and settle old scores. On one evening, police arrested Keith Ritson and Kevin McTaggart. The men were cruising around the west side in a vehicle that was camouflaged to look like an unmarked detective's car. Ritson and McTaggart had a pistol, shotgun and several maps in their possession. Circled on the maps were locations of the homes of several of Greene's targets, including that of Eugene Ciasullo, Allie Calabrese, and Joseph B. Kovach Jr., former Teamster and employee of a prominent firechasing company. Kovach was shot to death six days later. Nobody was ever charged in that murder or the attempted murder of Ciasullo.

In the meantime, news of Leo Moceri's murder buzzed through the twenty-four La Cosa Nostra families in the United States. That a family underboss could be killed by outsiders was an major embarrassment to the Cleveland mob.

"Nardi's the brains behind it," Tony Delsanter suggested to Jimmy Fratianno. "This guy's gone fucking crazy since Johnny Scalish died. You know, he was never made and it really pissed him off. They hit Eugene and Leo first because they're the ones they feared the most. Now we've got a war on our hands."

"You guys need some soldiers," Jimmy said. "How long since you've made anybody?"

"Oh, shit, Scalish never made nobody for years and years. We need some young guys, new blood, some good workers."

"How about Ray Ferritto? Jimmy suggested. "He's a good man. Want me to give him a call?

"You know Jimmy, he's a good friend of Ronnie Crab—Ronnie Carabbia. In fact, we had Ray at Mosquito Lake for one of our Fourth of July bashes. Yeah, give him a call. I'd like to talk to him."

Tall and thin, with salt-and-pepper hair, Raymond Ferritto was a bookie and professional burglar from Erie, Pennsylvania. Raymond entered the world of crime quite early. At age thirteen, he was convicted of burglarizing two gas stations and was sentenced to two years of probation. At age fourteen, Raymond was working at a bronzing factory when an accident caused the amputation of two of his toes. At age seventeen he left high school and joined the Marine Corps, but was discharged honorably a month later because of the injuries to his foot.

During his twenties, Ferritto was a bookmaker and vending machine route man in Erie. He was married in 1948, and fathered three children before he divorced in 1956. He remarried in 1957 and had one child. By that time Ferritto had moved to Warren, Ohio where he met Ronald Carabbia and Tony Delsanter. Carabbia was one of three brothers, all known as "Crab"—a play on their last name— who had become prominent in Youngstown-area organized crime. Delsanter was a made Mafia member and associate of the Licavoli family. He managed the Cleveland mob's gambling interests in the Mahoning Valley.

In 1958, at age twenty-nine, Ferritto was arrested for burglary. He plead guilty and served three years of a three-to-five year sentence. Once out, Ferritto spent some time in the Cleveland area where he committed several burglaries with Allie Calabrese and Pasquale Butchie Cisternino.

By the late sixties, Ferritto had moved to Los Angeles where he was associated with a group of Cleveland hoods which included Julius Petro. In the forties, Petro wriggled free from a death sentence on a retrial in a murder case. Ferritto and Petro were associates of Jimmy Fratianno, who by that time was on his way up the ranks of the Southern California Mafia. Likewise, Ray Ferritto was trying to make a name for himself.

In 1969, Ferritto booked a flight from Los Angeles to Erie. He was driven to the airport by another burglar, originally from Cleveland. Accompanying the two, just for the ride, was Julius Petro. The accomplice wheeled the car into an airport parking garage spot. Ferritto waited for a plane to take off, thrust a gun to the back of Julius Petro's head and pulled the trigger. The single fatal report was muffled by the roar of the jet. The murder resulted from a conflict with a well-known and successful bookmaker in Los Angeles who used Petro as a muscler. Ferritto and his accomplice were likely candidates for the contract, since they both disliked Petro.

Prior to the hit at the airport, Ferritto tried to plant a bomb on Petro's car. While assembling the explosive, Ferritto accidentally detonated the blasting cap causing a minor injury to his leg. He opted for the "one-way ride" method of execution next. Petro's killing went unsolved for years, until a dramatic turn of events began to unfold.

In 1971, Ferritto was convicted of burglary, this time with explosives. He was sentenced to fifteen years and incarcerated at Chino Penal Institution for Men in Chino, California. Jimmy Fratianno also happened to be doing time at Chino and the two became friends.

In 1974, Ferritto was released from Chino and returned to Erie. He started booking again and also worked for a vending company which was owned by a cousin. By that time, Ray developed an ulcer serious enough to require partial removal of his stomach. To calm his nerves, he took handfuls of antacid tablets and even smoked marijuana.

In May of 1976, Ferritto received a call from Jimmy Fratianno who was visiting in Warren, Ohio.

"I'm in Warren Ray. I'd like to talk to you. It's important."

The next day Ferritto drove to Warren and met with Fratianno in the cocktail lounge of a motel. Fratianno was with a west coast insurance agent paying $5,000 to meet with Jackie Presser. The three exchanged greetings and the insurance agent left.

"They're having some problems in Cleveland," Fratianno explained. "Somebody's trying to muscle in. I think you should talk to Tony [Delsanter]. You might be able to make some money with him."

"Yeah but what's in it for me?" Ferritto asked.

"Well if you're interested, I can set up a meeting with Tony and you can talk about it then."

Two weeks later Fratianno telephoned Ferritto in Erie and arranged a meeting. The next evening Fratianno, Ferritto and Delsanter met at Cherry's Top of the Mall Restaurant in Warren.

"You guys have something to discuss," Fratianno said. "I'll leave you alone."

Jimmy walked over and sat at the bar. Ferritto and Delsanter sat down at a table, exchanged amenities then lowered their voices to just above a whisper.

"Has Jimmy told you about the problems we're having Ray?" Delsanter asked.

"Just that somebody's trying to muscle in on the gambling."

"There's two," Delsanter explained. "John Nardi and Danny Greene and they've gotta be taken care of."

"I'm interested Tony but what's in it for me?"

"I'll have to ask Jack because he's the boss."

Greene was too big a prize for an exclusive murder contract. In the beginning, Ferritto was unaware that other attempts were being made to kill Greene and Nardi. They had become such a nuisance and threat to Licavoli that numerous mob associates were interested in killing them. It was assumed that the successful assassin would be greatly rewarded and gain instant respect in the underworld. Ferritto didn't hear from Carabbia or Delsanter for several months. In the meantime, the situation in Cleveland's underworld approached near chaos.

Before Ferritto could accept the contract to kill Greene and Nardi, Butchie Cisternino and convicted bank robber Allie Calabrese went after him. They tried to kill Nardi in Little Italy with a high-powered rifle. Another attempt was made a few days later when a shotgun blast was fired at Nardi from a moving car.

Nardi granted an interview to a reporter inquiring about a rumor that Licavoli and he were feuding.

"I'm not feuding with anybody," Nardi laughed. "That's ridiculous. Why would I feud with Jack White? The man is a friend of mine. I've known him all my life. Besides, what would we feud about? I could see if there was a million dollars in this town, but there isn't. What are you going to take over? Headaches?"

Nardi denied that Danny Greene worked for him. "We're just friends. I'm friends with everybody." Nardi was asked about friends and associates reputed to be in the Mafia. "The newspapers say they're in the Mafia. I don't know that. I never ask anybody their business."

Nardi knew there was indeed something to feud about. Whoever succeeded in taking over the Cleveland La Cosa Nostra throne, would inherit control of the billion dollar Teamster pension fund, and thousands monthly from the Las Vegas skim and gambling operations in Youngstown and Cleveland.

In the meantime, Nardi's word out on the street was quite different than the story he gave the reporter.

"Everyone who took shots at me is gonna go," he threatened.

After learning of the murder attempts on Nardi, Ray Ferritto phoned Ronnie Carabbia to find out what was happening with the plans they had made. Another meeting was set up and again Ferritto drove to Warren. Tony Delsanter, Ronnie Crab and Butchie Cisternino were there. Also present was John Calandra.

Other than having a one-entry police record, John Calandra was an unlikely figure to be involved in the mob's war with Greene and Nardi. Sixty years old and still working at his Collinwood tool and die shop, he was in poor health as was the small white poodle that he would often be seen toting around affectionately. Apparently, Calandra's close friendship with Licavoli was the basis for his involvement.

The men shook hands and sat down for a short meeting and then dinner.

"I've read there have been attempts on John Nardi. Is the deal still good?" Ferritto asked.

"It's still good," Calandra answered.

"Ray we've had problems getting a schedule on Greene and Nardi," Delsanter added. "Their moves are erratic and we can't pin them down."

"There's been a lot of people calling about Leo," Calandra said. "They want to know what's happening and if anything's being done."

The meeting ended with an agreement that Ferritto would assist in trying to get a schedule on Greene.

Two weeks after Nardi was shot at, Greene's men wired a bomb to the ignition of Allie Calabrese's Lincoln Continental. Calabrese lived on a quiet street in Collinwood and made a habit of parking his car at a neighbor's house since he didn't have a driveway. He left his key in the car in case it had to be moved. Up until this time, the mob's war with Danny Greene had been without innocent casualties. That ended when Calabrese's 50-year-old neighbor Frank Pircio got up to leave for work. Calabrese's car was blocking Pircio's so he hopped in the Lincoln to move it and was killed in a horrific explosion.

Not only were bombs being used in the Mafia war with Nardi and Greene, they had become a favorite weapon in Northeast Ohio gangland. It was about this time that Cleveland was dubbed "bombing capital of the United States" by a newspaper. The Bureau of Alcohol, Tobacco and Firearms was so inundated with blast investigations that they tripled their manpower in northeast Ohio.

If they do nothing else, they make people sit up and pay attention," Edward Whelen wrote for Cleveland Magazine. For, while Americans are becoming inured to street violence (whether they accept it or not), bombings, with their God-awful terror and indiscriminate destruction, retain their power to startle and shock—the last frontier of violence. A bombing is the ultimate violent act intended to kill, maim or warn. . . A bombing provokes headlines, regardless of the human or property destruction, because the act itself appears so aberrant and the possible shredding of flesh—innocent flesh—is so real.

A month after Frank Pircio was killed, Ronnie Carabbia telephoned Ray Ferritto and arranged another meeting at Cherry's Restaurant. The next evening, Ferritto drove to Warren where he met with Tony Delsanter, Jack Licavoli, Butchie Cisternino and Carabbia.

The men exchanged greetings, took a table in the bar area and spoke softly.

"Jack, Ray's interested but he wants to know what's in it for him," Delsanter explained.

"Don't worry Ray, we'll take care of you," Licavoli promised. "We can pay you one lump sum or we could make you. If you'll go to Detroit we'll make you and give you 25% of the Warren and Youngstown gambling profits. You won't have to worry about money for the rest of your life."

"Okay, when you're ready, call me," Ferritto said.

"In the meantime, Butchie will do the legwork," Licavoli added. "And if a chance comes up to get Ritson and McTaggart, hit them too."

Just as casually as that, the decision was made. Licavoli now had a proven killer to take care of John Nardi, the Irishman and his Celtic Club lieutenants. The four got up, took a table in the dining room and ordered dinner.

Chapter 30

In April of 1977, an explosion jolted residents of Collinwood awake. The bomb had been planted on the car of Mafia associate John Delzoppo. When police and fire units arrived, they found a white male lying dead next to the car. The body had massive damage to the head—it was obvious that the man had been at the focus of the blast. But further investigation revealed that the dead man was not Delzoppo. It was a Hell's Angel by the name of Enis Crnic. Crnic had reportedly been retained by Danny Greene to murder Delzoppo. Either Crnic detonated the bomb accidently, killing himself or someone with him set it off purposely. Only the person or persons in the red car that witnesses saw speeding from the scene seconds after the blast could answer that question. They were never identified.

Crnic's death posed a major problem for the Hell's Angels. For some time, the Mafia had been using the Angels as muscle, but now the Cleveland mobsters were furious. It was obvious that the bikers also accepted murder contracts against them. Licavoli ordered stern warnings issued and his men held a meeting attended by the Hell's Angel's president. The biker boss defended his club by explaining that they were not responsible for Crnic's actions because he was a former member at the time he planted the bomb. Despite distrust and finger-pointing by mob members, the explanation was accepted by Licavoli. But it was two years before the Hell's Angels were used for any mob contracts.

Instead, Licavoli decided to induct some new blood into his ailing outfit. Mafia protocol required that he get permission to make new members from the commission in New York.

Angelo Lonardo contacted Cleveland mobster Peanuts Tronolone at his Florida travel agency to arrange a meeting with "Fat Tony"

Salerno of the Genovese Mafia in New York City. Salerno had been running things for boss Frank "Funzi" Tieri, who was ill. Since the thirties, the Cleveland family had a good working relationship with the Genovese family and were therefore represented by them on the commission. The Genovese family also represented the Buffalo and Pittsburgh La Cosa Nostra families.

Licavoli and Lonardo flew to New York and met with Salerno. Licavoli explained the problem with Greene and Nardi and received permission to make ten soldiers.

Chapter 31

While on a trip to New York, Jimmy Fratianno updated Genovese mob family chief Funzi Tieri on the situation in Cleveland.

"Tell Jack if he needs any help to let me know," Funzi said.

"Thanks," Jimmy said, "I will, but right now they want to handle their own problem. I gave them a good man and on my way out here I stopped in Cleveland and we made two guys."

"Did you make good men?" Tieri asked. "You've got to protect yourself against worms who turn against you. Too many guys today will betray their family for one reason or another. Times have changed."

"Yeah, I think so. Tony Liberatore. When he was a kid, I think he was the wheel-man during a robbery where a couple cops got killed. He was only seventeen, and he did like twenty years, but now he's got a big job with the county. The other guy's John Calandra. He's got a tool and die shop in Collinwood and is real close with Jack. I've known both for years."

Liberatore spent two decades incarcerated at the Ohio Penitentiary and the London, Ohio Prison Farm for his involvement in the 1938 murders of Cleveland officers Virgil Bayne and Gerald Bode. He was paroled in 1958 by an acting governor and became active in Laborers Local 860. He quickly demonstrated his leadership abilities. In 1972, he was granted a full pardon and in 1975, Cleveland Mayor Ralph Perk appointed him to the Regional Sewer Board. By then, Liberatore had been elected as business manager for Local 860.

Chapter 32

Jeffery Rabinowitz, 32, a high school dropout, worked as a car salesman at Cross Roads Lincoln-Mercury. Fifty-two year old Kenneth Ciarcia was another salesman there. Stocky with a dark complexion, Ciarcia was successful at Cross Roads thanks to his close friend Tony Liberatore who sent him many customers.

Rabinowitz and his 29-year-old, blonde girlfriend Geraldine Linhart lived together and were to be married. Their plans for the future included a suburban dream house. But the purchase of the new home was being prevented by a land contract lawsuit filed against their existing house.

During a Christmas party for the dealership, Ciarcia made a point to meet Linhart. He had a keen interest in her because of her position as a secretary with the F.B.I.'s bank robbery squad. Ciarcia got Linhart alone and struck up a conversation opening with some comments about his inability to do people favors.

"You know Gerri, I'm fed up with everything. I used to have a lot of contacts but now I can't even get my son-in-law a job," he complained.

Linhart listened politely as Ciarcia rambled on for some time. Then his conversation turning to James Licavoli and Tony Liberatore.

"So what's going on at the F.B.I. with Jack White and Tony Lib, he inquired boldly?"

Linhart shrugged her shoulders.

"Why don't you check and see what you can find out," Ciarcia suggested. "I'm sure they'd appreciate knowing. Maybe Tony could return the favor by helping with this civil case that Jeff told me about. Lib knows a lot of people."

The prospect of getting some inside influence with her land contract case appealed to Linhart. But she knew the risk of getting into trouble at work was too great. Ten days went by and Ciarcia telephoned Linhart suggesting again that she come up with something on White and Liberatore. Linhart refused. Ciarcia pressed on, promising that she would receive help with her case. The conversation ended with Linhart saying she'd think about it. A few days later, Ciarcia called her back. Gerri made their conversation brief.

"There's volumes on those two," she reported.

"Well see if you can find out what's going on with them Gerri. Especially who's saying all those bad things about them."

The next day, Gerri Linhart left her desk in the bank robbery squad, retrieved an investigative report on James Licavoli, photocopied it and re-filed the original. She wrote *James Licavoli* at the top. That evening, she took the report copy to Ciarcia's house. He skimmed through.

"Gerri, tell me about the numbers in the report."

"The numbers refer to informants," she explained.

"Can you find out who the informants are?"

"Why?"

"Well we just want to find out who is talking about us."

"The F.B.I. uses numbers so the informants can't be identified," Gerri explained.

"What about this informant number 882SD?"

"The SD stands for San Diego but I would never be able to find out who that is," Linhart insisted. "I don't know what else I can do for you."

Ciarcia took the file, wrapped it in newspaper, then stuck it in an empty Fruit Loops cereal box. The next day, he took the box to work and placed it in a cupboard where he stored some of his personal belongings.

During the next few days, Ciarcia continued to phone Gerri asking for the identities of the informants. He promised that in return, her civil court case would be taken care of. Linhart was apparently growing more desperate about her case. A few weeks later, in an unprecedented breach of Justice Department security, she entered the top secret informant room of the F.B.I. and hand-copied a list of informants. The names were classified as "TE" or top echelon, the highest ranking of the federal informers. Among the names on the list were John "Curly" Montana, a suspected mob hit man and Teamster figure Tony Hughes. Another name on the list was Daniel J. Greene, with a code name of "Mr. Patrick" in parenthesis.

Linhart was still having second thoughts She kept the list without telling anyone while Ciarcia continued to call her.

"Your court case is being taken care of," he promised. "Do you have anything for me?"

Finally Gerri told Ciarcia that she did indeed have something for him. At his request she brought the list to Cross Roads Lincoln-Mercury where Ciarcia and Tony Liberatore were waiting.

"Where's the list?" Liberatore asked her.

"I don't like this whole business," she said. Lib tried to reassure her.

"Nobody is going to get hurt. I know a lot of people. Your court case is going to be taken care of.

"I don't like this," she continued. "I don't like the position I'm being put in."

Liberatore got up.

"I'll be right back," he said as he left Ciarcia's office.

A few minutes later he returned and offered Gerri $1,000 in cash. It was enough to ease her second thoughts. She took the money and gave Liberatore the stolen list of informants.

Liberatore copied the names onto a separate sheet of paper then burned Gerri's original list. In late September, Linhart lost her court case. She complained to Ciarcia who promised carpeting for the new house in exchange for their promise to fix the case. He arranged another meeting with Liberatore.

"We're here as a sign of good faith," Liberatore began. "You've been nice to us and we want to help you out."

"I need $15,000 for the new house," Gerri told Liberatore.

"I couldn't possibly give you that much money," Liberatore insisted.

"I never even wanted money, just to get my court case settled favorably," she reasoned, striking a nerve with Liberatore.

"Meet me back here in the morning."

The next morning, Linhart was waiting when Liberatore arrived. He extended a bulging envelope toward Gerri.

"Okay, here's the money," he said. "You can pay me back when your old house gets sold."

Linhart wanted payment for her services not a loan. But she was desperate. She reached for the envelope, but Liberatore hesitated.

"I just want to know if you're good for it," he asked.

"I am," she replied.

"Okay, I'll take your word for it."

Eugene "the Animal" Ciasullo, Mafia enforcer and first casualty in the mob's war with Danny Greene. (Bureau of Alcohol, Tobacco & Firearms Photo)

Tony "Dope" Delsanter, the Cleveland mob's Mahoning Valley boss. (Author's Collection)

The body of Hell's Angel Enis Crnic, partially visible under the driver's door. Crnic had been retained by Danny Greene to plant a bomb on the car of a Mafia associate when it exploded prematurely. (Author's collection)

Police survey the bombing murder scene of Danny Greene's partner, John Nardi. Nardi was getting into the car (not visible) next to the fence, when the vehicle next to it was blown up by a remote-controlled explosive.
(Courtesy of Cleveland Police Dept.)

The actual bomb box constructed by Mafia soldiers to murder Danny Greene in front of his girlfriend's apartment.
(Courtesy of Cleveland Police Dept.)

Danny Greene, shirtless and sporting his gold Celtic cross, looks more like a Celtic warrior than ever. He taunts the Mafia on television after the murder of John Nardi. (Courtesy of WJW TV, Cleveland.)

Mosquito Lake Resort. It was here on a boat where Mafia boss James Licavoli and his men planned the murder of the Irishman. (Courtesy of Lyndhurst Police Department.)

A police-constructed replica of the car door bomb box used to kill Greene. It was later used in court. (Courtesy of Lyndhurst Police Department.)

Overhead shot of Greene murder scene showing bomb car on left and the Lincoln that he was getting into. Danny's body is visible under right rear corner of bomb car. (Courtesy of Lyndhurst Police Dept.)

Murder scene of Danny Greene. Finally the Mafia had won their war with the Irishman. Or had they? (Courtesy of Lyndhurst Police Department)

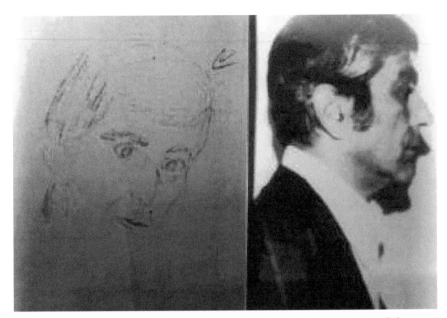

Raymond Ferritto, the Mafia associate retained to murder Greene - and the sketch made by an eyewitness. (Courtesy of Lyndhurst Police Dept.)

Mafia boss James "Jack White" Licavoli in his mugshot photo from the Danny Greene murder arrest. (Courtesy of Cleveland Police Dept.)

Dennis Kucinich, the Cleveland Mayor who was the subject of a Mafia assassination plot in 1978. Kucinich is a Congressman now. (Courtesy of Cleveland State University)

Thomas J. Sinito, Mafia lieutenant and suspect in the 1978 plot to kill Mayor Dennis Kucinich. (Courtesy of Lyndhurst Police Dept.)

Chuck Rini, mob associate missing and presumed dead. (Author's collection)

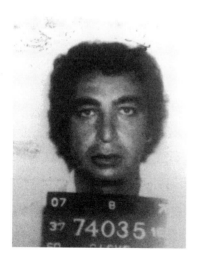

Jimmy Prato, Pittsburgh
mafioso in charge of Ohio's
Mahoning Valley rackets.
(Courtesy of the Vindicator)

Joey Naples, protege of Prato.
Murdered in 1991.
(Courtesy of the Vindicator)

James Traficant, the Mahoning County sheriff who was charged with accepting Mafia bribe money. Traficant was acquitted and later elected to Congress. (Courtesy of the Vindicator)

John LaRocca, longtime boss of the Pittsburgh Mafia.

(Pennsylvania Crime Commission photo)

Keith Ritson, chief enforcer for Danny Greene.

(Courtesy of Cleveland Police)

Hartmut "Hans the Surgeon" Graewe, vicious drug ring enforcer.

(Courtesy of Cleveland Police Dept.)

The body of drug ring victim and former Greene enforcer, Keith Ritson, after being pulled from an Ohio quarry.

(Author's collection)

Police and Navy divers removing the body of Joe Giaimo, (inset) one of numerous drug ring victims, from an Ohio quarry. (Author's collection)

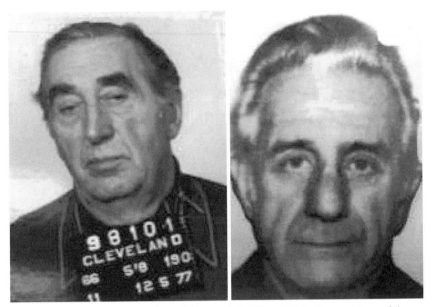

Angelo "Big Ange" Lonardo and Jimmy "the Weasel" Fratianno - two of the highest ranking Mafia members ever to become government cooperating witnesses. (Courtesy of Cleveland State University and Cleveland Police Dept.)

Anthony "Fat Tony" Salerno, boss of New York's Genovese crime family which represented Cleveland on the Mafia commission. He was convicted in the "commission trial," sentenced to life and died in prison. (Author's collection)

John "Peanuts" Tronolone, titular head of the Cleveland La Cosa Nostra during his 1989 arrest by Broward County (Florida) deputies. *Inset*: Broward Lt. David Green posing as an ex-Hell's Angel in the Tronolone bust.
(Photos courtesy of the Sun Sentinel)

Peanuts Tronolone, in his first mug shot. (Author's collection)

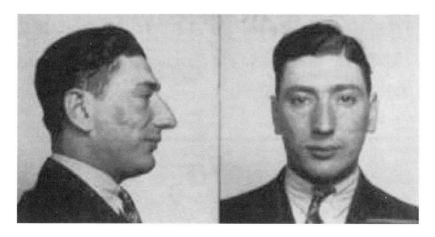

Joseph "Joe Loose," Iaccobaci (right), appears to be the dominant force of what remains on the Cleveland Mafia scene. His partner, Alfred "Allie" Calabrese (left) died in prison of natural causes in 1999. (Author's collection)

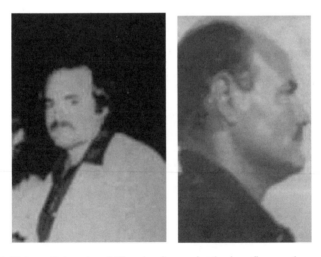

Tony P. Delmonti, low-level Cleveland organized crime figure who worked as a federal informant during the late 1990s - shown in a 1975 photo and a 1998 mugshot. (Author's collection)

Eugene "the Animal" Ciasullo (center), with friend Jimmy Martino (right) and the author, at a chance meeting during a Little Italy gathering in 1996. (Author's collection)

Ernie Biondillo, most recent victim of Northeast Ohio Mafia violence, and the car he was shotgunned to death in. (Photos courtesy of the Vindicator)

Lenny Strollo, Pittsburgh Mafia member most recently in charge of the
Mahoning Valley rackets. (Courtesy of the Vindicator)

Chapter 33

For years, Danny Greene had been searching for that one big score. This would be the racket to bring him power and big money. In 1976, the Drug Enforcement Administration had Greene under investigation for the suspected purchase of Phenyl Acetic Acid, which is used to manufacture methamphetamine or "speed." Following is an excerpt from the D.E.A. report.

On May 13, 1976, Group 63, New York Regional Office received information from R.W. GREEF & COMPANY that they had received an order for 551 pounds of phenyl acetic acid from RODCO, 421 Stone's Levee Road, Cleveland, Ohio. A bank check for $1267.30 accompanied the order. . . . [name deleted] stated he believed that RODCO was owned by DANNY GREEN and that the phenyl acetic acid was destined for a clandestine "speed" laboratory. [name deleted] further stated that GREEN was a labor organizer in the Cleveland area and was involved in organized crime. . . RODCO had ordered approximately 50 pounds of phenyl acetic acid one year ago, but that order had been cancelled.

Apparently Greene abandoned his plans under the heat of the D.E.A. investigation. In 1977, he and John Nardi struck gold together. They began working on a joint venture in which they would take over a financially ailing cattle ranch in Texas, and sell the meat through a discount purchasing program for labor union members.

The ranch owner, Richman Harper, had been indicted, but acquitted on charges of conspiring to sell explosives to Cuba. Heavily in debt, he was likely to go bankrupt. Through Nardi's underworld connections, he would have the purchase locked up. He'd arrange for the financing and Greene would be his point man.

The meat would be sold through cooperative outlets across the nation, and a laborer's union membership card would entitle him to a generous discount. It was going to be the same set-up unions used to provide their members with other discounted services or products like medical insurance or low-cost eye glasses. It would be a major money maker—and better yet, legal. Relocating to Texas would also end their problems with the Mafia, and free them from the bitter Cleveland winters. Danny was even preparing with some custom made western wear—complete with green cowboy boots and hat.

Greene had Columbus attorney Donald Eacret form an umbrella company for the deal. It was to have a Gaelic name—Micuarata Corporation—meaning "mountain in which my treasures are stored."

Eacret would later say that the numbers would have never worked for Greene and Nardi.

"Greene and Harper projected annual sales of $6 million over a five-year period," Eacret explained. "But it would have taken $7 million just to refurbish the feeder lot and plant. And that does not include buying new cattle."

Like most of the lawyers Danny hired, he never paid Eacret for his legal work. He claimed that the publicity attorneys received from representing him, was more than enough compensation.

For the meat deal, John Nardi planned to seek financing from Paul Castellano, boss of the Gambino mob clan in New York City. Castellano had decades of experience in the meat industry. Tony Milano set up an appointment with Castellano for his nephew, and Greene and Nardi booked a flight to New York.

Their plans to relocate to Texas were not happening fast enough. Butchie Cisternino and another man, said to be Allie Calabrese, got wind of the travel plans and rented a hotel room overlooking the parking lot at Cleveland's Hopkins International Airport. They waited for Greene and Nardi to leave for New York, then planted a bomb on their car. The bomb was controlled by a remote detonator. It was a perfect set-up. When Greene and Nardi returned from New York and got into their car, Cisternino and Calabrese would be watching from their hotel room window and trigger the explosive with the remote control. With the pressing of one button, the Mafia's worst headache would be over.

On March 14, 1977, Nardi and Greene returned from their two-day trip to New York. Allie had been watching with binoculars and spotted the two men walking toward Greene's car. Butchie readied the remote control and layed his thumb gently on the button. Nardi went around to the passenger side and Greene unlocked the driver's door. When both men closed their doors, Butchie pressed the button.

Nothing. Butchie pressed the button again. Nothing. He pressed it numerous times. Still nothing. Nothing but the sound of a jet taking off and a view of Greene pulling out of the parking spot.

"Son of a bitch!" Cisternino muttered and bolted for the door. "We're not close enough Allie. C'mon!"

The two ran to the hotel stairwell and started quickly down the eight flights of steps while Greene cruised out of the lot, headed for the parking toll booths. When Cisternino and Calabrese reached the ground floor, they opened the door to the lobby and ran toward the hotel exit as several curious bystanders looked on. Repeatedly, Butchie pressed the detonator. By this time, Greene and Nardi were out of view and at the parking toll booth.

"Your total is seven dollars," the attendant said.

Greene handed her a $10.00 bill.

"Keep the change, he said."

"Thank *you* sir."

Chapter 34

On May 17, 1977, after three attempts on his life, John Nardi was killed by a Mafia car bomb. Despite having Raymond Ferritto looking to kill Greene and Nardi, Jack Licavoli had also assigned hitman John "Curly" Montana to hunt down Nardi. The F.B.I. maintained that Montana and another individual murdered Nardi. The bomb car system was reportedly set up by Butchie Cisternino.

Police believe the third participant was Henry "Boom-Boom" Grecco, a mob associate and aptly-nicknamed bomber. He was believed to be shot and killed several weeks after Nardi was blown up. Investigators received information that Grecco was murdered for failing to manufacture a bomb. The explosive was to be used to kill a bar owner who was resisting the efforts of Cisternino and his crew to get their own vending machines placed there. Grecco's body has never been found.

In the wake of John Nardi's murder, his family members refused to admit that he had any ties to organized crime.

"Johnny was always helping somebody," his uncle Tony Milano explained to a reporter. "The F.B.I., the C.I.A., the police. The newspapers made him out to be somebody he wasn't. He was just a union man. He didn't bother nobody. He was no Mafiosi."

Nick Nardi, John's brother and a respected labor leader added: "John's death is the direct result of news stories about him. The stories built him up to be somebody to get out of the way. He was not involved in anything. He was always helping people, getting them jobs."

Shortly after Nardi's murder, Danny granted an interview to reporter Bill McKay who worked for WJW TV. He trusted the journalist because of his Irish-American background. Flanked by several

Celtic Club representatives, Danny stood shirtless—his Celtic cross gleaming in the sunlight. His arms were crossed defiantly, and he looked more like a Celtic warrior then ever before. He answered McKay's questions confidently.

"Rumor has it Danny that the word was out on the street back in March that John Nardi was a target," McKay said. "Did you talk to John Nardi at all about this?"

"I haven't personally seen John in about three-and-a-half months Bill, but I did send him a message very recently that John, be careful, it's out here very, very strong on the streets that somebody's out to get you. Now from what I can see is that everybody says they heard this also. The investigators should start right there and go from who told you and where did they hear it from."

"Do you have any thoughts about where these people are from?"

"I think most probably the bomb was made here—the people could have been imported."

"Word has it Danny that you are also a target in this so-called gangland war for control. What's your answer to that?"

"In the world of the streets I happen to have a very enviable position to many people because I'm in between both worlds, the square world and the street world and I think I have trust in both sides. I have no axe to grind, but if these maggots in this so-called Mafia want to come after me, I'm over here by the Celtic Club. I'm not hard to find."

Licavoli, Calandra and the rest of the Cleveland Mafia hierarchy and their admirers were incensed. Did this brazen bastard have any idea of who he was dealing with? Did he have a death wish?

Chapter 35

One week following Danny Greene's bold, televised challenge to the Mafia, Tony Delsanter, the Cleveland mob's Youngstown representative, died unexpectedly. Ronnie Carabbia would eventually take over Delsanter's responsibilities. Jimmy Fratianno travelled from San Francisco to Warren, Ohio for the funeral. During the wake, he, Jack Licavoli and mob soldiers Ray Ferritto and Butchie Cisternino discussed the Greene murder contract.

"If you need anything Ray, see John [Calandra] and he'll get it for you," Licavoli said.

Ferritto was upset that he was using his own credit card to pay for a hotel room. He complained that he had no car to drive and that he wasn't getting any help from anyone.

"I need money for expenses," he insisted.

"I don't know Ray. I'll see what I can do to get it to you." Licavoli said. "And when this thing is over we'll make you and you'll get 25% of what's coming out of Youngstown and Warren."

Licavoli pulled Fratianno aside and showed him the stolen list of F.B.I. informants. The Weasel had good reason to be very nervous. For almost a decade, Fratianno had been an F.B.I. informant in California. He scanned the list.

"This is great Jack. Can she get information like this from California? You know we've got some stoolies out there."

"I don't think so Jimmy," Licavoli replied. "Not unless it's got something to do with Cleveland."

When Fratianno returned to Los Angeles, he phoned his F.B.I. contact who worked out of the San Diego field office. He told him about the list of informants stolen from the Cleveland office. Fratianno just wanted him to contact the Cleveland agents to inform them of the leak. At first, the agent didn't believe him.

"Check it out yourself," Fratianno urged. "Two of the names on the list were Tony Hughes and Danny Greene."

Hughes was Jackie Presser's right-hand man.

"If it's true than it's an historic breach of F.B.I. security. There would be many people whose lives are in danger with a leak like that," the agent said.

"Yeah, no kidding. So just call them and have 'em plug the leak.

"Jim, it's not that easy. This could turn out to be very big. We'll need detailed information—you'll have to go back to Cleveland to get more for us. And eventually, you'll have to testify."

"No way."

Jimmy's F.B.I. contact was adamant about Fratianno getting involved, but Jimmy continued to refuse. The agent forwarded the little information he had to the Cleveland agents. At first, they too could not believe there was such a monumental leak in their office, until they were provided with the names of Hughes and Presser.

The Cleveland F.B.I. had a mole in their midst. They began investigating but had little to go on. That was until they got an anonymous call from a man requesting to meet with them.

Chapter 36

In June of 1977, Raymond Ferritto drove his 1974 Cadillac from Erie, Pennsylvania to Cleveland. It was the first of numerous two to three-week-long trips that Ray would made to gather information about Greene. Usually he stayed at a Holiday Inn or Sheraton Inn. Butchie Cisternino provided Ferritto with a list of license plate numbers and descriptions of cars that Danny used. He also gave him Cleveland Magazine issue which contained an article entitled *The Bombing Business*. The story included photographs of Greene and Nardi. For a time, Ferritto even lived in the same apartment building in which Greene was living with his girlfriend.

In nervous drives in and around Collinwood, Cisternino showed Ferritto Danny's trailers on Waterloo, his girlfriend's apartment building on Lakeshore Boulevard and the Kenny King Restaurant that Greene frequented. But Danny remained an elusive target. For months, Ferritto and either Butchie Cisternino or Ronnie Carabbia cruised Collinwood, trying to spot the Irishman.

But Greene remained an elusive target. He surfaced when he attempted to make peace with Licavoli. Danny made the cease-fire offer through Frank Embrescia, a senior mob member and friend of Frank Brancato, who had died a couple of years earlier. Licavoli's terms were that Greene's lieutenant—Keith Ritson—be sacrificed for his supposed role in the murder of Leo Moceri and the attempted murder of Eugene Ciasullo. Danny flat out refused.

Believing that such an atmosphere of peace might relax the cautious Irishman, Licavoli reluctantly agreed to a plan devised by Jimmy Fratianno. The scheme would involve the Gambino soldiers who had loaned Shondor Birns the $70,000 that in turn was loaned to, and lost by Greene. They too were interested in justice. A meeting was held between Fratianno, Licavoli, the Gambino soldiers and Danny. It was decided that Greene could temporarily take over gambling operations on the West Side of Cleveland. This would allow a cease-fire and also give Danny the opportunity to repay the loan from the Gambino family.

Shortly after the meeting, Greene and his men quickly moved in on a large West Side gambling operation that was originally run by John Nardi. Danny offered Licavoli a percentage, but he declined. He didn't want money from Greene—he wanted him dead.

While Danny Greene let his guard down a bit, informal meetings to plan his murder continued to be held at Butchie Cisternino's apartment in Collinwood. Allie Calabrese and Ronnie Carabbia would be there to discuss plans. On occasion, John Calandra showed up carrying his white poodle.

By early September, Ferritto and Cisternino decided on a plan of action. They would set up a remote-controlled bomb in the bushes near the front door of Danny's apartment and detonate it when Greene walked by.

To increase the effectiveness of the explosive, Cisternino had a steel box constructed to direct the blast. The bomb would be placed in the box which would be secured into the ground with railroad spikes—the open side of the box facing the target area. The explosive itself included a large plastic jug filled with gasoline and nails to act as shrapnel.

In the meantime, Tony Liberatore assembled a team of his own to kill Greene. He retained two ex-cons, one of whom was a paroled killer. He provided them with guns and a car—ironically an old police cruiser.

"If you pull this off, you won't have to worry about a thing," Liberatore promised the men. "This thing has gone on long enough. Jack White wants this done. You gotta get it done. You get this thing done and you can write your own ticket in this town."

On September 24th, the F.B.I. had their Title III surveillance equipment intercepting a conversation inside Licavoli's house.

LICAVOLI: Johnny Nardi. That cock sucker. And this fucking Irishman.

CALANDRA: How the hell did this guy ever come into the pic-
ture?
LICAVOLI: Everybody's around him. You can't get near him. . . If
he says he'll be there at three o'clock, fuck it, who gives a shit.
You wait, you wait and wait and then you get tired of waiting.
He don't keep no time.
CALANDRA: He's no dummy.
LICAVOLI: Yeah like the game that Nardi opened on the West
Side. Boy did the Irishman want to give me a piece. I don't want
nothin' from that sonavabitch.
CALANDRA: He's got to screw up some time.
LICAVOLI: Oh he's got to make a mistake. I hope he goes back to
Texas so they can kill him there.
CALANDRA: Where Jack?
LICAVOLI: Texas. Them cocksuckers on the west side, they all go
with him. You know, McTaggart and all them.

The following week, Ronnie Carabbia called Ferritto and told him
that something had come up. The two men met at Carabbia's vending
machine company. From there they drove forty minutes to Mosquito
Lake, a private boating resort and picnic area halfway between
Cleveland and Youngstown. At the gate, they were greeted by Jack
Licavoli, John Calandra, Butchie Cisternino and Angelo Lonardo.

The men boarded an eight-sleeper luxury boat and went into the
enclosed cabin. The boat was owned by a physician, a friend of
Licavoli. There they listened to a cassette tape recording made from
the tap on Greene's phone. Of interest was the following call made by
Greene's girlfriend.

RECEPTIONIST: Dr. Candoli's office, may I help you.
WOMAN'S VOICE: Hi, I'm calling for Danny Greene.
RECEPTIONIST: Okay
WOMAN'S VOICE: He has a loose filling and uhm, would like to
see Dr. Candoli as soon as You can get him in.
RECEPTIONIST: Alright, let me see what we have available.
[pause] We can squeeze him in on this Thursday—that's the
sixth at three o'clock, will that work?

WOMAN'S VOICE: That'll be fine.

RECEPTIONIST: Good, then we'll see Mr. Greene on the sixth at three o'clock.

WOMAN'S VOICE: Thank you.

RECEPTIONIST: You're welcome, have a nice day.

Licavoli, Lonardo, Calandra, Ferritto and Cisternino smiled at each other.

"Butchie says he knows where this Dr. Candoli's office is," Licavoli announced.

"Yeah—he's in an office building in Lyndhurst," Cisternino informed.

Knowing in advance again when and where Danny Greene would be might be the answer to their lack of success in killing the Irishman. The men discussed this latest development and it was decided to use a bomb car to kill Danny when he arrived for his dental appointment.

"Kind of funny," Licavoli chuckled. "He's going to the dentist to get a loose filling fixed."

The men all laughed.

Chapter 37

On Wednesday, October 5, 1977, Ray Ferritto drove to a suburban apartment owned by a friend of Cisternino. Cisternino was there and Ronnie Carabbia arrived an hour later. The three men walked outside and Cisternino showed them the "Joe Blow" car, a maroon Chevy Nova registered to a fictitious named and outfitted with a special steel bomb compartment welded into the passenger door. The three went back up to the apartment where they talked, ate and watched television into the evening. Cisternino left. Carabbia and Ferritto spent the night at the apartment.

The next morning Cisternino returned with a brown, paper shopping bag. Inside the bag was a police scanner and the components to make the bomb: a nine-volt battery with alligator clips, blasting caps, the remote control detonator and three sticks of dynamite wrapped in brown wax paper. Butchie layed the parts on the table and with Ferritto's help began carefully and methodically assembling the bomb. They finished in an hour.

The explosive and receiver were held in a cigar box with an inner switch to make contact when the remote control was triggered. There was also an outside safety switch to activate the whole package and prevent the possibility of an accidental detonation. The remote control detonator was actually a device used to fly model airplanes. It was an eight inch square plastic box housing a lever, meter and telescopic antenna. Cisternino placed the assembled bomb in one shopping bag and the remote control in another.

At 2:00 P.M., an hour before Greene's scheduled dental appointment, Ferritto and Ronnie Carabbia left Winchester Hills Apartments with the bomb car and the getaway car. Cisternino stayed behind to monitor the police radio. The afternoon sun shone bright and warm as the two men made their way south on Interstate 271, twenty minutes to Exit 32 at Cedar and Brainard Roads in the bedroom community of Lyndhurst.

Carabbia casually pulled the bomb car into the parking lot of the six-story Brainard Place Medical Building and immediately parked it near the lot entrance. He got out, walked over to where Ferritto had parked the getaway car to get a good view of the whole lot and the main entrance. Carabbia got into the car with Ferritto and the two hitmen began the wait for their target.

Fifteen minutes later, Tony Liberatore's backup hit team arrived in their old police car—the emblem outline still visible on the door. The rifle supplied to them lay on the back seat wrapped in the same piece of flowered cloth it was picked up in. A .357-Magnum revolver lay under the passenger seat. They pulled next to Ferritto and Carabbia.

"Well what do you wanna do, shoot him or blew him up?" one of the back-up team asked,

"Well there might not be a space for the bomb car, so if you guys get a clear shot, then shoot him," Carabbia instructed. Liberatore's men agreed and moved their car to the opposite side of the parking lot where they too would have a clear view of the main entrance.

It was now 3:00 P.M., and Greene was nowhere in sight. They all waited, Ferritto and Carabbia rather calmly and the back-up team rather nervously.

At 3:15 P.M., Greene had still not shown up. Carabbia and Ferritto chatted about the likelihood that Greene had once again eluded them.

"Wait. Isn't that him, Ray?" Carabbia asked, pointing toward a brown Lincoln pulling in the lot.

"Yeah, yeah that's him," Ferritto confirmed. "That's Ritson's car he's in."

For several months Danny had been switching cars with Keith Ritson as a tactic to avoid detection. The back-up team also saw Danny enter the lot and readied their high-powered rifle. Danny steered the big Lincoln into a parking slot, then pulled forward into the adjoining, empty space for an easy exit. He grabbed his green, leather gym bag from the passenger seat. The bag was somewhat of a portable survival kit that Danny had been toting around. Inside was a Browning 9mm semi-automatic pistol, capable of firing fifteen rounds without reloading, an extra clip of bullets, a list of car license plate numbers of several of Licavoli's soldiers, a box of green ink pens and a Mother of Perpetual Help holy card.

Danny exited the car, locked the doors and started walking rather quickly toward the building entrance. Greene's old friend Billy McDuffy was supposed to watch the Lincoln while Danny was at the dentist. Before he left for his dental appointment, Greene paged McDuffy, but he never got the message because the batteries in his pager were dead.

Danny was already twenty minutes late for his appointment as he disappeared inside the lobby. A few minutes later, the back-up hit team pulled next to Carabbia and Ferritto.

"We didn't shoot because we think there's somebody in another car watching Greene," one of them explained.

"You guys go ahead and leave, Carabbia told them. "Ray and I will stick around and use the bomb car."

As the two back-up men left, Ferritto pulled the bomb car through the lot and backed it in next to Danny's car so it was facing the same direction. Ever so delicately, he placed the bomb package inside the steel bomb box along with a large package of nuts and bolts. Ferritto switched the remote control receiver on, replaced the steel box cover and tightened down the nuts. He spread a green blanket over the top of the bomb box to hide it from outside view. Whether Ferritto and Carabbia chose a green blanket as a sarcastic joke, or by accident, was never learned. Ferritto got back into the Plymouth with Carabbia and pulled out to the street, stopping off the road. From a phone booth there, the two had a good view of the front entrance as they waited for Danny to exit the building.

Inside Brainard Place, Danny went to the third floor office of Dr. Dominic Candoli and checked in with the receptionist.

"I'll be right back," Danny said.

"Okay Mr. Greene," she replied.

Danny left the office, took the elevator going back down to the lobby and walked to a pay phone. He called his son Danny Jr. with instructions to bring his eyeglasses to a restaurant in Collinwood.

"I'll need them to sign the papers for the big meat deal," Danny explained.

Danny returned to Dr. Candoli's office and was ushered to a dentist chair. Candoli appeared a few moments later, greeted Danny, then the two exchanged pleasantries. The dentist worked on Danny for roughly fifteen minutes, chatting cheerfully as he repaired the loose filling. After Dr. Candoli completed the work, the two men said good-bye and Danny checked out with the receptionist.

"Good-bye," he said.

"Have a nice day Mr. Greene."

Danny smiled back at her.

Minutes later Greene emerged from the building walking, as if preoccupied toward his car. Ferritto hopped in the driver's seat of the Plymouth and started cruising away slowly. He turned right toward the entrance to Interstate 271. With bomb transmitter in hand, Carabbia watched intently from the back seat as the Irishman approached his car.

◆   ◆   ◆

"I thought the boiler blew up," recalls a school teacher.

"A construction accident I figured," a cop running radar a mile north on Interstate 271 recollects.

Inside Brainard Place, stunned doctors, dentists, nurses, receptionists and patients rushed to the windows to investigate the boom that caused the floor to tremble momentarily.

At the Lyndhurst Police dispatch desk, the first call came in as a car fire. The fire department was given the assignment and one police unit was routinely dispatched to assist. Moments later phone calls started flooding the switchboard and additional police and fire units began speeding toward Brainard Place.

The bomb car was demolished and the Lincoln was severely damaged. The remote-controlled explosive had found its mark. Standing only inches from the steel-box encased bomb when it exploded, Danny Greene was killed instantly while reaching to unlock his car door. There was much horrific damage to his back but his body was left largely intact except for his left arm which was blown almost one-hundred feet away. His prized emerald ring was still attached to a finger.

Police and bomb squad technicians conducted an extensive and exhausting search of the scene. They located and cataloged hundreds of pieces of the bomb, including bits of circuit board from the remote control, blasting cap wires, scraps of electrical tape and battery casing fragments.

Greene's body landed face up just under the rear end of the bomb car. Like an impromptu memorial, his gold, Celtic cross was imbedded in the asphalt a few feet away. Danny might have explained that he died proudly, without fear, facing the man upstairs. After at least seven attempts on his life, the Irishman was dead. Danny's strings had finally been pulled and his coveted guardian angel had been powerless to intervene. Live by the Sword. Die by the Sword.

Chapter 38

Several days after Danny Greene's murder, the F.B.I. intercepted some interesting conversation through their Title III surveillance at mob boss Jack Licavoli's Little Italy house. Apparently Licavoli, his right-hand man John Calandra and an unidentified male were complaining about Greene's brazen behavior, and about mob figures Frank Embrescia, Frank Brancato and John Nardi. They felt that these men, as well as the F.B.I., were responsible for the Irishman's rise to power.

LICAVOLI: Embrescia was so fuckin' burned up when Shondor got it. Oh don't tell me about that. Hey if he couldn't handle that bastard, that's his own fault.

CALANDRA: That's right. That's right.

UNIDENTIFIED: How can a marked man put a big flag in front of his house. He had a big Irish flag out by the side, anybody could see it. He put it there on purpose. He'd be sitting out there under the sun.

CALANDRA: He has some pretty good connections though.

LICAVOLI: He had some connections all right. The fuckin' F.B.I. He used to tell them about every goddamed thing everyone did.

CALANDRA: You know that with Greene. He was the F.B.I.'s boy.

LICAVOLI: Oh fuck yes. But he didn't work with the F.B.I., he told them what to do!

CALANDRA: Sure, you're right.

LICAVOLI: He told them what to do. He said F.B.I. your ass. He thought he got so fuckin' big.

UNIDENTIFIED: Right

LICAVOLI: Well he wanted it all that's all. Him and Nardi. That fucker. He used to give them the money and he used to give them all the information. He created a monster.

CALANDRA: Nardi and Brancato.

LICAVOLI: That's right. They created that guy. And all the fuckin'
headaches we used to have.

Licavoli didn't know then but his headaches were just beginning.

Ronnie Carabbia and Raymond Ferritto never saw them. The two
hitmen were too focused on watching for Danny Greene to reach his
car. But moments after the bomb exploded, a young woman and her
husband noticed Carabbia in the back of the getaway car. It was a
strange sight. It was no taxicab, but there was the driver and one passenger in the back. Like the young couple, the two men were glancing
back repeatedly at the cloud of smoke, dust and debris while cruising
toward the freeway on-ramp. But the mis-seated pair did not seem
shocked at the blast.

Once on the interstate, the young couple took notice of the blue
Chevrolet again as it passed them. This time there was no rear passenger.

"He must be laying down on the seat," the husband said.

As Ferritto passed by, the young woman got one quick look at his
face.

Lady luck was holding neither Greene's nor Licavoli's hand that day.
The odds were probably one million to one but Raymond Ferritto's mug
had just been recorded in the alert mind of an artist. And being the
daughter of a policeman, she was sharp enough to instruct her husband
to copy down the Pennsylvania license plate number.

When the couple arrived home, the woman immediately telephoned her father and gave him the license plate number. Then she sat
down and drew a sketch of the man driving the blue Nova.

A mammoth investigation had just gotten off to a rocket start. The
woman's father turned the sketch and license plate number over to
investigators Andy Vanyo, Rocco Poluttro and Ed Kovacic of the
Cleveland Police Intelligence Unit. Ferritto was already known in the
C.P.D. Intelligence Unit and the sketch was such an accurate likeness
that they were able to identify him immediately.

In the meantime, the newspapers were screaming with headlines
like "Car bomb kills Danny Greene." Television news programs
repeatedly aired footage from the blast site, including grisly shots of
the Irishman's severed arm.

Chapter 39

Only a few days after Danny Greene was killed, one the most effective and far-reaching cooperative efforts was begun in law enforcement. A strike force of various agencies was amassed to solve the historic Mafia hit. They included the Cleveland Police Department, Lyndhurst Police Bomb Squad, the Federal Bureau of Investigation, the Bureau of Alcohol, Tobacco and Firearms, the Pennsylvania State Police and the U.S. Attorney's Office. The Cuyahoga County Prosecutor appointed two attorneys to work exclusively with the strike force. It was a monumental case. Detectives of the Lyndhurst Police Department interviewed 600 people.

Investigation began with the getaway car license plate number and was aimed at Raymond Ferritto. A check of license applications revealed that the bomb car and the getaway bore sequential registration stickers. They had been applied for together and the applications bore the same handwriting. The strike force now had both cars linked together.

A search warrant was executed at Ferritto's house in Erie, Pennsylvania. Some interesting items were confiscated from the house including the Cleveland Magazine issue that had been provided to Ferritto. It was found opened to the article containing Greene's photograph. The most incriminating evidence was found in Ferritto's Cadillac. There, stuck in the visor, investigators located the registration papers to the getaway car.

An arrest warrant was issued for Ferritto. His photograph was flashed on television news shows and published in numerous Midwest newspapers. After hearing that he was being described as armed and dangerous, Ferritto surrendered to police in Pittsburgh and was extradited to Cleveland.

Raymond Ferritto waited patiently in jail. He was hoping that

Licavoli would supply a good attorney for him. He hoped wrong. Instead, Ferritto got wind that there was a murder contract on his head. If the mob got rid of Ray, there would be nobody to testify against the others. Ferritto was appalled by their treachery.

"All my life I've been one way," he later said. "I always did what I was supposed to do and now all of a sudden I did them the biggest favor that they wanted done and they were talking about killing me and here I am in jail awaiting trial. . ."

The mob had forced his hand. Ferritto had only one way out. He made a deal with the feds.

"It wasn't because I saw God or read a bible. It was just that I thought at that time that I had to look out for me. . . And I thought that would be my best move."

In addition to revealing everything he knew about the Greene murder plot, Ferritto was required to plead guilty to the 1960s murder of Julius Petro in Los Angeles. After several weeks of debriefing Ferritto and preparing affidavits, the strike force divided into teams to execute the warrants. Licavoli was arrested at home. His cane, with the long hidden blade was immediately confiscated. Agents located $3,000 in cash inside the don's underwear drawer.

Lonardo was also apprehended at home. At his request, agents let him change his clothes for the trip downtown. He put on a suit and tie. His wife offered the agents coffee and cookies while they waited. They declined.

Calandra was picked up at his Crown Tool and Die Shop in Collinwood. On the way to F.B.I. headquarters, the unmarked car was hit from behind by another vehicle causing minor damage. Detectives and F.B.I. agents jumped out of their cars with guns drawn thinking the accident might be a ruse to free their prisoner. Calandra complained of chest pains. He was taken to a hospital, examined and released then taken back to F.B.I. headquarters.

Cisternino and Calabrese were both arrested without incident at their respective homes.

Sinito was taken into custody at a friend's house.

In North Miami Beach, Florida F.B.I. agents apprehended Ronnie Carabbia at a motel. He was registered there under the fictitious name of Crown, perhaps a reference to Calandra's tool and die shop.

In San Francisco it was 2:40 P.M., when F.B.I. Special Agent Jim

Ahearn met with Jimmy Fratianno at a motel to execute an arrest warrant charging the Weasel with aggravated murder.

In the meantime, Cleveland F.B.I. agents were still looking for leads in the theft of their files. They received a call from a man who refused to give his name. He said he thought he had something that belonged to the F.B.I. and wanted to meet with an agent. When F.B.I. agents met with the man, he handed them a grocery bag.

"I think this belongs to you. I put it back together just like I found it."

The man was the owner of Cross Roads Lincoln-Mercury. Inside the bag was a cereal box. Inside the box was a stack of papers wrapped in newspaper. It was the stolen file on Licavoli.

"I was so happy I could've kissed the guy," the agent later said.

At F.B.I. headquarters, agents examined the file copy from Cross Roads. A handwritten notation on the first page was compared against dozens of samples from various F.B.I. employees. They got a match when they checked it against secretary Gerry Rabinowitz' handwriting. The agents couldn't believe it. It was a bittersweet finding. They were fond of Gerry and thought of her as a most loyal and dedicated co-worker. But fingerprint results confirmed it.

Before the agents approached Rabinowitz, they salted their current list of informants. They took some names off and added other names of organized crime figures who were not informants. They hoped to create confusion with any underworld characters who viewed their list.

A few weeks later, the agents approached Rabinowitz. They barely started questioning her when she broke down crying.

"I knew you guys would eventually get me," she sobbed. "I'm so glad it's over.

In a plea bargain, Rabinowitz agreed to cooperate with the F.B.I. and testify against Ciarcia and Liberatore. Arrest warrants were issued and Ciarcia was arrested. Liberatore could not be located and eventually was placed on the F.B.I.'s Ten Most Wanted List.

Only a week earlier, he had been questioned by a reporter with rumors that he was under investigation by the F.B.I.

"People like me are often subject to these kinds of things," Liberatore commented. "You know, I came up from nothing and I'm involved in a little politics and I run my local. . ."

Chapter 40

As the historic Danny Greene murder trial got underway, Raymond Ferritto testified that Butchie Cisternino detonated the bomb. Later he recanted his testimony.

"I was upset with Butchie for supplying me with a getaway car that could be traced," Ferritto explained.

Ferritto was a star witness, but circumstances had produced a turncoat far more damaging than him. Jimmy Fratianno was already on the run from west coast mobsters who correctly suspected him of being an informant. The charge of conspiring to kill Danny Greene put him over the edge. F.B.I. agents convinced him that only way out was to join WITSEC and becoming a cooperating witness. It was an unprecedented success for law enforcement. He had decades of experience in the Mafia and had been close with many bosses. A $100,000 bounty was immediately placed on the Weasel's head. Fratianno's 1978 defection presaged the decline of the Italian-American Mafia.

It was a marathon trial—79 days—making it the longest continuous criminal litigation in Cuyahoga County history. One-hundred and twenty-nine witnesses testified. Four hundred pieces of evidence were presented to the jury including replicas of the car door bomb box and the remote control bomb—wired to ring a bell and flash a light remotely, from 100 yards away.

But in the end, only Cisternino and Ronnie Carabbia were convicted. Allie Calabrese had been discharged for lack of sufficient evidence and all of the others were acquitted.

Cisternino's alibi failed him. A friend testified that he called Butchie from a certain phone booth during the time that Cisternino was supposed to be assembling the bomb. The friend told the court that Butchie was at home, making spaghetti sauce. The plan backfired when Cleveland Police Intelligence Sgt. Rocco Poluttro checked out the phone booth that the call was allegedly made from. An investigation with Ohio Bell Telephone Company representatives revealed that the phone booth had not been installed until one week after the call was supposedly made. Cisternino's friend was convicted of perjury.

The confusing finding by the jury that Greene's murder was not part of an organized crime battle also contributed to the acquittals. Lyndhurst Police Chief Roger Smyth couldn't figure it.

"What was the jury thinking?" he asked reporters in frustration. "Do they think Carabbia and Cisternino killed Greene just for the hell of it? Certainly this was a murder for hire."

But Chief Smyth still looked on the bright side.

"I'm not going to say all our efforts were for naught. We did get Carabbia and Cisternino. We got Ferritto and Fratianno to plead guilty. We got one of Liberatore's back-up team to plead guilty. We got the other one to plead guilty after he was arrested while looking for Brian O'Donnell. We also got the Rabinowitzes, who stole some F.B.I. files, to plead guilty to helping the mob. And we got a car dealer to plead guilty to forgery. That's nine people convicted from one gang bombing."

Cisternino's defense attorney was bitter over his client's conviction.

"If they didn't believe it was a murder for hire with gangland overtones, then why convict anybody?" he argued. "If nobody paid to have this done than what sense does it make to think that two men would kill Greene for no reason. It was a compromise verdict, plain and simple."

One prosecuting attorney explained that the jury had trouble believing Ferritto and one of the back-up hit men who flipped—both men being convicted killers. Other investigators were very soured that Licavoli and the other top mobsters weren't convicted.

"They just wanted to get off as cheaply as possible," an F.B.I. agent said. "I think their total cash outlay in this thing was $5,000. If the mob brought in some real professional and done the job right it would have been another unsolved bomb killing."

One Cleveland Police detective agreed and lambasted the outfit.

"They could have killed Greene easily, often, if they had just walked up to him with a shotgun and let fly. . . They didn't want to face him man to man. Danny would have scared them up a tree, even if he wasn't armed. . . The Cleveland mob is cheap. That's all there is to it. There's money here, but they must all bury it in their backyards in tomato cans. . ."

Chapter ⟨41⟩

After the Danny Greene murder trial ended, the U.S. Marshal's Service and F.B.I. began hauling silver-haired Jimmy Fratianno across the country to testify in major mob cases. One of the first was the R.I.C.O. trial of Frank "Funzi" Tieri, boss of the Genovese mob group in New York. Tieri was convicted and given a long sentence.

Fratianno had provided much intelligence against the Southern California La Cosa Nostra, which had been under the leadership of Dominic Philip Brooklier (ne Bruccoleri). In early 1980, Brooklier was indicted along with his underboss Sam Sciortino and three underlings. In November, the men were all convicted of various racketeering charges. They were acquitted of the most serious charge, the murder of Frank "Bomp" Bompensiero, a mobster and F.B.I. informant. Fratianno was a key witness in the trial. Brooklier was sentenced to four years in prison.

The Southern California then came under the control of Peter Milano and his brother Carmen, the sons of Cleveland mob figure Tony Milano. The F.B.I. and other law enforcement investigators were progressing well in their fight to bring that family down. They had two informants working with them. The two men, brothers Larry and Craig Fiato, were soldiers in La Cosa Nostra. Their disloyalty to their former mob friends weighed heavily on the brothers. They were interviewed by Kim Murphy, staff writer for the Los Angeles Times.

"Everytime you put that wire on, you die. . . ," Larry related. *"I mean these are guys you've grown up with, that you've admired all your life. . . You're seein people from the past."*

"You're seein' your father who may be turnin' over in his grave, lookin' at you," Craig added. *"You're seein' guys that knew you as a kid, that came to your father's wake and gave an*

*envelope to your mother, that looked out for your family. . .
You gotta get pain from that. . . I mean, when I was a kid and
I saw Mafia guys walk down the street, I'd look up at these
guys and, oh my God. I'd get such a great feeling when they'd
just acknowledge me."*

Beginning in the early eighties, the F.B.I. began building another
case against the Southern California La Cosa Nostra. At the time,
Peter Milano was doing well in his efforts to organize loan sharks and
bookmakers. Milano had the clout and smarts to organize the fledgling west coast rackets.

"Pete Milano was a man with a purpose," Craig Fiato said.
*"He had all the experiences of everybody behind him. He knew
everybody that was runnin' between the raindrops, and who
didn't follow through, who hesitated, who'd been involved with
stool pigeons and so on. And he was really bulking up his crew.
You talk about ambition. He had Caesar's ambition."*

In March of 1988, after two weeks of intense negotiations, Pete
and Carmen Milano and five of their underlings, pleaded guilty to various racketeering charges. They never admitted any ties to La Cosa
Nostra.

U.S. Attorney General Edwin Meese called it the most significant
organized crime prosecution on the West Coast in more than a decade.

Prosecutor Richard Small announced, "we indicted what we
believe to be the hierarchy of the La Cosa Nostra family in Los
Angeles. "We have effectively put them out of business. This is it. This
is the family."

Law enforcement officials nationwide often punctuated their
notable mob convictions by declaring the Mafia to be dead. Roughly
ten years later, the L.A. crime family was put out of business again. A
dozen convictions followed an investigation stemming from the 1997
murder of "Fat Herbie" Blitzstein, whose street operations had been
targeted for takeover. Blitzstein was a lieutenant of Anthony Spilotro,
the Chicago mob representative in Law Vegas who was portrayed by
actor Joe Pesci in the hit mob movie, *Casino.*

PART 4
The Aftermath

Primary Characters

♦ Charles "Charlie Crab" Carabbia: *Cleveland Mafia figure stationed in Youngstown, Ohio*

♦ Jimmy "the Weasel" Fratianno: *Mafia captain*

♦ Joe Gallo: *Mafia lieutenant*

♦ Hartmut "Hans the Surgeon" Graewe: *Drug ring enforcer*

♦ Dennis Kucinich: *Mayor of Cleveland; future Congressman*

♦ James "Jack White" Licavoli: *Mafia boss*

♦ Angelo "Big Ange" Lonardo: *Mafia underboss*

♦ Joey Naples: *Pittsburgh Mafia figure stationed in Youngstown, Ohio area*

♦ Jimmy Prato: *Pittsburgh Mafia underboss stationed in Youngstown, Ohio area*

♦ James Traficant: *Popular sheriff acquitted of taking Mafia bribe; future Congressman*

♦ John "Peanuts" Tronolone: *Cleveland mob figure living in Florida*

♦ Carmen Zagaria: *Drug ring leader; Mafia associate*

Chapter 42

A few months after the murder of Danny Greene, Kansas City F.B.I. started applying for Title III court-authorized secret listening devices which were installed at various locations where members of Kansas City's Civella Mafia family conducted business. What they discovered had much farther reaching consequences then they ever imagined. In time, the investigation was dubbed "Strawman."

Allen R. Glick had been a law student at Case Western Reserve University in Cleveland. He graduated in 1967 after completing his undergraduate work at Ohio State University. Glick settled in San Diego and became involved with a real estate development and investment company called Saratoga Development Company. Glick was intrigued by a proposition to purchase a Las Vegas casino. After acquiring financing, he became lessee of the Hacienda Hotel and Casino.

An opportunity then followed for Glick to buy the Freemont and Stardust Hotels/Casinos. To make the deal, he needed $62 million. Glick had previously met Al Baron, executive director of the Teamsters Union Central States Pension Fund. The pension fund was established in 1955. Members of the Teamsters, mostly truck drivers, taxi drivers and warehouse workers, pay a cut of their weekly paycheck into the fund toward their retirement. The money is invested by the board of trustees who are appointed by the national Teamsters president. The first major Las Vegas loan was to Moe Dalitz for construction of the Sunrise Hospital.

Baron was not very supportive but referred Glick to Frank Ranney, a fund trustee from Milwaukee. Ranney instructed Glick to meet with Milwaukee mob boss, Frank Balistrieri.

To get Glick's loan approved, Balistrieri sought the support of Kansas City Mafia boss Nick Civella. In 1973, Civella talked to

Chicago mob heads and asked Cleveland rackets figure Maishe
Rockman if he could arrange for the loan through the Teamsters pension fund. Rockman, through his influence with Ohio Teamster boss
Bill Presser, helped get the loan approved. Ironically, at the same time,
F.B.I. informant and Teamster leader Jackie Presser was providing the
government crucial background information on the Mafia's casino
skimming system and key players.

Glick, age 32, created a holding company naming it Argent
Corporation—(A)llen (R) (G)lick (ENT)ertainment. By 1975, Argent
had acquired ownership of several more major Las Vegas hotel/casi-
nos—the Fremont, the Marina, and the Stardust. Glick was ordered to
put Frank "Lefty" Rosenthal in charge of the casinos. Rosenthal,
along with enforcer Tony Spilotro, were assigned by Chicago mob
chiefs Tony Accardo and Joe Aiuppa to monitor their Las Vegas interests. Rosenthal was paid $250,000 a year. He held various titles, such
as Food and Beverage Director and Entertainment Director, positions
that did not require licensing by Nevada's Gaming Control
Commission. It wasn't long before Glick tried squaring off with
Rosenthal, threatening to fire him. Rosenthal was quick to put him in
his place.

"I was told not to tolerate any nonsense from you because you are
not my boss Allen. And if you don't do what you're told, you'll never
leave this corporation alive."

Shortly thereafter, it was learned that the Argent casino finances
were a mess. Many people were stealing from the casino and giving
kickbacks. In June of 1976, Carl Thomas was hired by Nick Civella to
straighten things out. Carl Thomas was an executive at Circus Circus
Hotel/Casino when he began his skimming career. Thomas became
C.E.O. of Glick's Argent Corporation through the influence of Allen
Dorfman. Dorfman was on the board of the Teamsters' Central States
Pension Fund and was close with Chicago Mafia figures. Dorfman was
also partners in Almagamated Insurance which processed claims for the
Teamsters Central States Health and Welfare Fund.

After investigating the financial status of the Argent casinos, Carl
Thomas reported back to Civella.

"It's like a bucket with twenty holes in it Nick. The money is going
every which way. There's no control over it."

In didn't take long for Thomas to take control of the casinos. By the fall of 1976, the only persons stealing from the casinos were those under the supervision of Thomas, who in turn was under the control of the Kansas City Mafia. During a two-month period late in the year, Thomas was able to skim $80,000 from the casinos.

In 1977, Joe Agosto became the producer of the Tropicana's popular Folies Bergere show. Chicago had representation in Las Vegas with Lefty Rosenthal, their inside man, and Tony Spilotro, their outside man. Now Kansas City had Joe Agosto as their man in Nevada.

Agosto was the immigrant who reportedly took the name that was used by the son of Porrello sugar war partner Black Sam Todaro. In 1929, 8-year-old Joseph Todaro was sent to Italy after his father was gunned down by Angelo Lonardo, in revenge for the murder of Lonardo's father. Renamed Joseph Agosto, Todaro's son died mysteriously twenty years later.

A few months later, Sicilian Mafia figure Vincenzo Pianetti, born in Italy in 1927, took the name Joseph Agosto and emigrated to the United States. Agosto eventually settled in Kansas City with the Porrello family, cousins to Cleveland's Prohibition-era racketeer brothers. One member of the Kansas City Porrellos was a member of the Civella Mafia group. Apparently, it was through Agosto's relationship with the Porrellos and his own past history, that he became prominent in the Civella family.

In 1978, the Mafia pressured Allen Glick into selling the Stardust. Kansas City mob underboss Carl "Tuffy" DeLuna personally delivered a chilling warning to Glick.

"You might think of your life as expendable," DeLuna explained. "But you might not think of your children's lives as expendable. If I don't hear about the announcement to sell immediately, your sons will killed one by one."

DeLuna then read off the names and ages of Glick's sons.

Glick replied anxiously, "I assure you Mr. DeLuna I will sell."

Glick reportedly sold 50% of Argent to two of Frank Balistrieri's sons. The men reportedly paid Glick $30,000.

When the Strawman indictments came down, F.B.I. agents convinced Joe Agosto to testify against Civella and the other K.C. and Chicago mobsters. Though Agosto died before testifying, the F.B.I. still had the intelligence he provided and other significant evidence like the seizure of incriminating records kept by Carl Deluna.

Before the case went to trial, Nick Civella died. He had been the Kansas City mob boss for thirty years. After a nine-month trial, the other Chicago and Kansas City racketeers, some twelve men were convicted. They included Carl DeLuna, Carl Civella, Carl Thomas and Anthony "Stompie" Chivola, a Chicago cop and nephew of the Civellas.

But it wasn't over yet. The F.B.I. was busy preparing to bring down additional, related indictments in a case they called Strawman II. And they would have a powerful surprise witness, courtesy of the mob's war with Danny Greene.

Chapter 43

In 1978, Cleveland's 31-year-old Mayor Dennis Kucinich was in the middle of a political battle with the corporate community over the city's Municipal Light Plant. Five banks were refusing to renew the city's $15.5 million in short term notes unless Kucinich sold the 73-year-old light plant to the privately owned C.E.I.—Cleveland Electric Illuminating Company. The boyish-faced Kucinich knew that compromising on the public owned light plant would greatly damage his political base of support. He refused to sell and faced national embarrassment on December 16, 1978, as Cleveland went into financial default.

In the fall of 1978, Ed Kovacic, then a Cleveland police lieutenant, was contacted by the Maryland State Police and told that they had uncovered a plot to assassinate Mayor Kucinich. The murder contract was apparently put out because Kucinich had caused considerable problems for dishonest businessmen, politicians and criminals. The Mafia had eliminated two hurdles—Danny Greene and John Nardi—and now they were apparently hoping to eliminate another. Kovacic and Acting Police Chief Edwin Nagorski were able to confirm that a Cleveland organized crime figure, whom they had identified only by the first name of Tommy, had ordered the hit through an intermediary source in Baltimore.

The Baltimore intermediary relayed a message for the hired killer to visit Cleveland for instructions. He was to be paid $25,000 when Kucinich was dead. The murder had been planned for the week of October 9th, but Kucinich had been unexpectedly admitted to the hospital for an illness, so the plans were postponed.

As the investigation continued, Maryland authorities were able to discover that Tommy had an uncle named Joey Maxim, who was a former lightheavyweight boxing champion from Cleveland. A search of the Cleveland police files found that Tommy Sinito, lieutenant of Mafia underboss Angelo Lonardo, was related to Maxim and fit the physical description provided by the Maryland officials.

In December of 1978, the Maryland State Police learned that the murder had been rescheduled to occur between Christmas and New Years, and that the hitman would again be visiting Cleveland for instructions. The meeting was to be held in the evening of December 27th, at a restaurant and bar called the Port of Call, located in Mayfield Heights on Cleveland's east side. Plainclothes officers staked out the meeting and saw the hitman enter the bar. His presence was acknowledged by Sinito with a nod of his head. Apparently Sinito knew he was being watched because no other contact occurred between the two men. Shortly thereafter, the hitman left Cleveland. Kucinich lost a re-election bid and presumably, the murder plans had been called off. There was never enough evidence amassed to indict Sinito, or his mob bosses.

It would be years before the truth about Cleveland going into default would be known. It has been called the "corporate overthrow of an elected official," and a "flagrant move to interfere with the democratic political process." Kucinich called it a "swindle," a case of the bank and corporate community attempting to force the sale of an important city asset as a price for credit. A congressional study later found that 70 directors and officers of the banks which refused to renew the city's credit, had contributed to an earlier recall effort against Kucinich.

In the end, Dennis Kucinich was vindicated," wrote journalist Michael Drexler for the Cleveland Edition in 1988. "Selling Muny Light to C.E.I. was not the key to solvency, as his adversaries had declared. Soon after default, in 1979, the public did have a chance to decide on both his proposed tax increase, and on the fate of Muny Light. They took on the tax hike, and refused to give up Muny Light to C.E.I. When George Voinovich became mayor, he became a Muny Light advocate. Though default labeled Cleveland as a bad credit risk for years, the city is now deemed a good bet. And Muny Light remains publicly owned, and also in good shape.

Chapter 44

Carmen Zagaria was a burly ex-high school football player who became a carpenter. Later, he bought his own floor covering company. Zagaria's ambition and business acumen may have served him well had he stayed in that field. But in the seventies, he began dealing drugs on a small scale. In 1979, he bought a tropical fish store called the Jungle Aquarium, which served as a meeting place and front for his narcotics operations. At home, he kept a Doberman Pinscher for protection. He named the dog "Al Capone II."

Not long after the murder of Danny Greene, mob lieutenants Joey Gallo and Tommy Sinito became involved with Zagaria's drug operation. Reportedly, they received the blessing of Mafia bosses Licavoli and Angelo Lonardo. Gallo operated his mob business out of a front company called Shoppings Our Service or SOS on Chagrin Boulevard. Nearby was Developers Unlimited, run by reputed Mafia associate, Sam Vecchio. Both spots were frequent gathering places for racketeers like Moe Kiraly, Ronald Bey, Kevin McTaggart, and Keith Ritson. After the death of their leader, McTaggart and Ritson joined the Zagaria drug ring. In a strange twist of events, they became associates of the same men they had been fighting.

Zagaria's chief enforcer was a brutal German immigrant named Hartmut "Hans" Graewe. Graewe delighted in dismembering his victims to discourage easy identification. Thus he was nicknamed "Doc" and "the Surgeon." He kept a hacksaw and butcher knife in a bag that he referred to as his "tools." His car, an old Volkswagen van was his "ambulance."

Graewe was a greatly feared figure in the drug underworld. He was arrested for stomping his wife to death in a bar. During his incarceration for the murder, Graewe was put in a cell with three blacks.

Immediately they started giving him a hard time.

"We're in charge here white boy," one announced.

"Yeah, don't say shit mother-fucker," another threatened.

The black prisoners had picked on the wrong white boy. Graewe grabbed one of them and slammed him so hard into the cell bars that he broke the man's back. When the other two jumped on Graewe he kicked one in the face, shattering his jaw. The third black prisoner retreated and stood in disbelief as his friends lay moaning on the cell floor.

Graewe turned to him and asked, "whose in charge now?"

"You are," the man replied.

Reportedly, the charge of murdering his wife was eventually dropped when nobody would agree to testify against Graewe.

Chapter 45

By 1980, the Zagaria-Gallo drug operation had grown to include at least twenty couriers. They were paid $1,000, plus expenses, per trip and flew into Florida by commercial aircraft. The large amounts of cash were stacked in luggage in a manner to avoid detection by airport x-ray machines. While in Florida, the drug runners rented cars, and paid for all expenses in cash, to avoid the paper trail created by credit cards.

The Zagaria-Gallo partnership was making a fortune. But all of the money wasn't enough to avoid resorting to murder. There seemed to be no end in sight for the violent killings. In a two year period, there were seven men who were murdered as a result of clashes with Zagaria, Gallo and Graewe. One significant case was Joseph Giaimo.

Giamo was a drug wholesaler who worked out of a hotel he owned in North Bay Village, Florida. He was closely associated with the Cleveland Mafia family and mobsters in Florida and New York City. Joey Gallo instructed Zagaria to make his wholesale drug buys from Giaimo whenever possible.

In 1980, Carmen Zagaria purchased ten 1,500 pound loads of marijuana, 13 pounds of cocaine and 600,000 Qualudes from Florida supplier Joe Giaimo. But dealing with Giaimo became increasingly difficult because he was cheating on his drug sales. Zagaria accused him of using too much packaging paper or wetting down the marijuana, both methods of inflating the weight. Giaimo also substituted candy tablets for significant amounts of Qualudes .

Despite Zagaria's mistrust of Giaimo, the two men began socializing and became friends. Giaimo opened up to Zagaria and told him of grievances he had with Sinito and Gallo.

Zagaria reported the remarks to Sinito and Gallo.

RICK PORRELLO

"Joe offered me to go in partners with him. He wants to cut you two out."

Sinito and Gallo were angry and started talking about killing Giaimo. The men decided to murder Giaimo but first planned to steal a shipment of drugs from him. In early January of 1981, Zagaria sent a convoy of drug runners to Florida to pick up 1,900 pounds of marijuana from Giaimo. On the evening of January 17th, Giaimo agreed to meet Zagaria at the fish store to get paid for the marijuana. When he got there, he and Zagaria started arguing. Giaimo became suspicious and drew a revolver from his waistband.

"Don't fuck with me Carmen," he warned Zagaria.

Hans Graewe had been hiding in the fish store. He sneaked up on Giaimo and shot him several times in the back of the head. Giaimo died instantly.

Zagaria didn't think he could get Giaimo's body out of the store without being noticed. So he and Graewe decided to dispose of the body right in the basement of the fish store. Using brick and mortar they actually sealed the body in a wall building a makeshift crypt.

◆　　◆　　◆

Carmen Basile was a senior made member of the Mafia and owned the Golden Anchor Inn and Restaurant on the West Side. Like Joe Gallo, Basile felt that Zagaria should be inducted into the Mafia.

"You had been doing all this good work. . ." Basile told Zagaria. "You did Joe Giaimo. . . I have to go to Angelo Lonardo, and I have to tell him what happened, and you should be respected in the United States as all members are. You should become a member and Angelo should be proud."

Zagaria replied, "I don't want to be involved. I am involved enough. Just forget about it."

It seemed that a chaotic spree of killings and pressure were getting to Zagaria. But the cold-blooded killer Hans Graewe thought this would be a good opportunity for his boss to take over everything.

"After you learn where everything is coming from, I'll blast all of them," he suggested. "I'll kill Licavoli and Lonardo first. I'll put them in my van and mix them up so nobody can figure out who's who."

In March of 1981, there was another murder. Gallo and some of the others invested their drug profits in loose gems—presumably to avoid creating a taxable trail. Gallo had a close friend named Chuck Rini, who often assisted in the transportation of the stones. On April 1st, Rini's car was found near Gallo's office. Rini has not been seen or heard from since. Investigation has suggested that he might have been killed in a conflict with a jeweler.

Chapter 46

On a chilly evening in December of 1981, Carmen Zagaria and Hans Graewe met at the fish store. They decided that they had to move Joe Giaimo's body. Together they smashed a fifty-pound weight against the brick and mortar tomb. After several minutes they were able to pull the hideously decomposed corpse free. Zagaria, gagging and ready to vomit from the stench, tried holding his breath as he and Graewe lifted the body to the trunk of a waiting car.

Zagaria and Graewe headed for Jacquay Quarries, a remote area outside of Cleveland. They intended to dump Giamo's body in a pond there. One of their drug couriers followed in another car to help. About a quarter of a mile before they reached the pond, Zagaria's car ran out of gasoline. They pushed the car to the pond while the drug courier went for gas.

Zagaria opened the trunk, recoiling again from the odor. After Giamo's body was lifted from the trunk to the ground, Graewe grabbed a tire iron, raised it and started beating in Giamo's skull. Zagaria took hold of the iron and yanked it away.

"Enough is enough!" he shouted. "Let's just throw it in the water."

Zagaria and Graewe lifted the body, swung it twice and threw it into the pond. The body splashed in the murky water and disappeared. A few seconds later it popped to the surface. In daylight it would have been in plain view of passers-by.

"What should we do now?" Zagaria asked Graewe. "We're out of gas and Joe Giamo's body is floating in the water."

Both men waited. After an hour, the drug courier had not returned so Zagaria left on foot with the hope of finding a gas station. He stopped at a bar and called another one of his drug couriers to bring gas. The man arrived an hour later along with Graewe who had hitched a ride in the back of a pickup truck.

"I'm freezing," Graewe said. "Let's not go back yet."

Then three men sat down and Zagaria bought them a round of beer. After twenty minutes they headed back to the Quarries. The drug courier brought his bottle of beer with him. They put gas in Zagaria's car but it would not start because the battery was dead.

The drug courier looked up the road.

"Shit! There's a cop coming," he shouted.

Zagaria and Graewe ran behind a tree and concealed themselves in the dark. Graewe pulled out a .38 revolver. The lone police officer pulled up and exited his car. Graewe, a crack shot, centered the revolver's sights on the officer's head.

"What's the problem?" the officer asked the drug courier.

"Oh I'm just out of gas," he replied. "But I've got a friend coming to help."

The officer seemed suspicious of the story and started shining his flashlight around. The beam of light swept passed the pond and Giamo's floating body. He walked over to the door of car and peered inside. He reached in and pulled out the bottle of beer.

"You know I can arrest you for this," he rebuked the courier sternly. He handed the bottle to him. "Pour it out."

"Yes sir," the courier replied, emptying the beer on the shoulder of the road. The policeman recorded the man's name in his notebook then left. Afterward, the three men obtained some twine from a Plain Dealer newspaper delivery man who was parked a little down the road. Standing knee deep in the freezing water, they tied several heavy rocks to the body and watched it drop into the darkness. They returned to Cleveland.

A few days later, Zagaria and Graewe returned to the Quarries with two manhole covers. They waded into the water, pulled the corpse to the surface and wired the manhole covers to it. The body quickly sank to the bottom of the pond and they started driving back toward Cleveland. Still not satisfied that the body would remain submerged, they turned around and returned to the pond. They struggled with the body until they got it to the surface then floated it toward a deeper section of the water. There they secured the manhole covers and several rocks to it and let it sink.

In the meantime, Joey Gallo was continuing his attempts to recruit Zagaria into the Mafia. He believed that Carmen's ambition would bring new life to the Cleveland family. Gallo explained to Zagaria how the Cleveland family had weakened in membership over the years, resulting in a lack of experienced, strong leadership. That is until Angelo Lonardo took over as head of the Cleveland Mafia after Jack Licavoli was indicted for racketeering in connection with the murder of Danny Greene.

"See, there should be, like, people between us. Know what I mean Carmen? But they didn't do nothing for all those years over here. Just let it go dormant. . . See Angelo's probably one of the most respected guys in the whole United States. . . He's really the kind of guy we needed in this town a long time ago. . . But he's gonna be seventy. We're missing the guy that's sixty. And we're missing the guy that's fifty. It's all the way down to me at forty. That hurts us, see?"

Gallo told Zagaria that he expected to take over leadership of the family and that Tommy Sinito would be second-in-command.

"Join us Carmen and you can be in charge of a crew of soldiers," Gallo promised. "I'll be the boss and Tommy will be second-in-command. You'll be an underboss and have guys under you."

"I'm involved deep enough," Zagaria lamented. "I don't want to join the Mafia."

A few days later, mob members from Florida and New York arrived in Cleveland, looking for Giaimo and the 1,900 pounds of marijuana worth a half million dollars. They met with Tommy Sinito. He pointed them toward Zagaria but warned them not to kill him because of the large amount of money he owed the "old timers," referring to Licavoli and Lonardo.

The men contacted Zagaria and arranged to meet him at a Howard Johnson's Motel. Fearing they would try to kill him, Zagaria had his gang members reinforced by a half dozen members of an outlaw motorcycle club. The bikers arrived in their black leather and chain regalia and seated themselves in the restaurant near Zagaria. The New York and Florida mobsters were not happy.

"I don't like that you brought all these bikers here, Carmen. It insults me," one of them said.

They interrogated Zagaria about the disappearance of Joe Giaimo and the marijuana but he kept insisting that he knew nothing.

Eventually they sympathized with him.

"We realize that you're caught in the middle and taking the blame for Tommy Sinito," one allowed. He offered Zagaria a deal. "We'll keep shipping Carmen but charge you at an inflated rate until we recoup the five hundred grand."

"I'll think about it," Zagaria replied, and the meeting ended.

Zagaria stalled the out-of-towners for several days, and they finally left.

Chapter 47

The Mahoning Valley, including Youngstown and Warren, Ohio, once flourished as part of America's industrial heartland. But in the sixties and seventies, the economy soured with the pressure of foreign competition and steel plant closings. The area became a haven for organized crime. During the sixties, there was so much political corruption and so many bombs exploding to settle mob disputes, that the area was dubbed Crimetown, U.S.A. and Bombtown, U.S.A. Police referred to car bombings as "Youngstown Tune-Ups."

"Organized crime here is a lucrative business because of the sizeable millworking population which provides a ready clientele for its services and goods," explained Cleveland Strike Force leader Steve Olah. "Add to that the political corruptibility, and it's a natural—almost like taking candy from a baby."

Former Youngstown attorney and San Francisco 49ers president Carmen Policy further added, "this is a working-class area and gambling is not considered a vice. In fact, gambling permeates everything. For its size, I admit, there is no city in America like Youngstown."

For decades, Sebastian "John" LaRocca was the La Cosa Nostra boss who controlled the rackets in Pittsburgh, western Pennsylvania and a section of the Mahoning Valley in Ohio. Gabriel "Kelly" Mannarino of New Kensington, Pennsylvania, rose through the ranks to become LaRocca's underboss. LaRocca, Mannarino and Michael Genovese attended the famous 1957 Mafia conference in Appalachin, New York.

According to the F.B.I., part of the Pittsburgh-Cleveland conflict in Youngstown began in the sixties, when Frank Brancato forced a successful Youngstown vending machine operator to cut the Cleveland family in for one-third of his profits. To insure continued profits, Brancato had enforcers work to bring the vending man new customers. When the man's competitors became resentful, bombings and shootings followed.

It was after the damaging publicity of the bombing murder of Youngstown gangster Charlie Cavallaro, his 8-year-old son, and maiming of another son, that both factions called a truce and agreed on territorial boundaries. Warren and Trumbull County, and Struthers in Mahoning County went to Cleveland and was put under the control of Tony Delsanter and the Carabbia brothers. Youngstown and the rest of Mahoning County would be Pittsburgh territory, under the supervision of Jimmy Prato. The cease-fire and apportioning of turf stayed in effect until the late seventies.

Prato was known as "Briar-Hill Jimmy" after the old mill district that he grew up in. He was born in Calabria, Italy, and his uncle was reportedly one of the Youngstown area's earliest organized crime bosses. Prato was a slight, balding man who spoke with a heavy Italian accent and attended church regularly. He was a powerful figure with influential connections. His attorney was Don Hanni, chairman of the Mahoning County Democratic Party and a member of the election board. For years, Prato had been investigated for running "the bug," nickname for the local numbers game.

His headquarters was his popular, neon-lit Calla-Mar Manor Restaurant located near an Ohio turnpike interchange. There, behind closed doors, he conducted business meetings at the center table of the dining room. It was above this table that the F.B.I. was able, under federal Title III authority, to place a hidden listening device. When the roof began leaking from faulty installation of the bug, Prato's men discovered the hidden microphone and ripped it out. The F.B.I. agents listening from a nearby undercover vehicle immediately moved in to recover their expensive equipment. But for several tense hours, Prato refused to surrender the equipment and even had the audacity to order his security guard to arrest the F.B.I. agents for trespassing. The part time security guard just happened to be the local police chief. He resigned as chief several days later.

Finally, additional agents were dispatched to the scene and surrounded the restaurant. They were instructed to arrest anyone causing interference while another agent was dispatched from Cleveland with a court order which was used to force the return of the F.B.I. equipment. When a reporter questioned Prato a few days later, he denied that the incident occurred.

"I run a good business," he insisted. "I have a fine restaurant and banquet hall. No such thing happened in my place."

After Ronnie Carabbia was imprisoned for the murder of Danny Greene, all hell broke loose in Warren and Youngstown. Carabbia had managed the interests of the Cleveland Mafia in that area. His incarceration created an opportunity for the Pittsburgh mob to move in. As a result, more than a dozen men were killed.

In late 1989, the Pittsburgh La Cosa Nostra tried moving into Cleveland territory. Running an impressive gambling operation were several Pittsburgh La Cosa Nostra associates. $10 million to $15 million in wagers per year were taken in by gamblers who bet on numbers that would appear in the Ohio and Pennsylvania state lotteries and the Wall Street Journal. With the success that law enforcement had from convictions in the murder of Danny Greene, the F.B.I. wasn't about to let organized crime gain a foothold in the Cleveland area. In September of 1992, the three men were indicted for federal gambling charges. They were all convicted and sentenced to 18 months to 21 months in prison.

Through the mid 1990s, the Pittsburgh La Cosa Nostra continued operating under the leadership of Michael Genovese. Sports-betting, numbers, barbut, video poker machines and drugs continue to be the main money-makers. Genovese delegated much of his operation to Charles "Chuckie" Porter and Louis Raucci. In 1990, Porter and Raucci were both sentenced to 27 years in prison. Raucci died in 1995. Reportedly, Thomas "Sonny" Ciancutti inherited their operation. Ciancutti had begun his career in the rackets as a protege of Kelly Mannarino.

Chapter 48

In 1980, it looked like the long-entrenched Youngstown racketeers were in for more trouble. James Traficant (ne Traficante) was a former star quarterback from the University of Pittsburgh who became a community activist and drug counselor, then decided to run for sheriff of Mahoning County. He was the underdog in a reform platform calling for "honesty in politics."

"It's time to stop rubber stamping the patronage and political deals. Together we can strike a blow against political bosses," Traficant asserted.

When Traficant was campaigning, the Cleveland Mafia decided to buy him off. The Carabbia brothers gave Traficant $100,000. Pittsburgh mobster Jimmy Prato and his protege Joey Naples wanted in on the payoff and gave Charlie Carabbia $60,000 to deliver to Traficant. Charlie had been running Cleveland's portion of the Mahoning Valley rackets ever since his brother Ronnie had been imprisoned for the bombing murder of Danny Greene. Charlie and his brother Orlie sat down with Traficant at the home of the Carabbia's mother. As an insurance policy, Charlie Carabbia concealed a pocket tape recorder on his person.

As part of a lengthy conversation between the two mobsters and Traficant, discussion was held regarding certain politicians who were allegedly controlled by the Pittsburgh Mafia. Traficant believed the number of crooked Mahoning Valley representatives was high.

ORLIE CARABBIA: "You really believe they got all them fucking people?"

TRAFICANT: "Yeah. . . Yes I do. . . I don't know all of them, but I know it's a fucking fistful. . . Now where's [Mahoning County

Prosecuting Attorney] Vincent Gilmartin? Does Gilmartin sit with you?

CHARLIE CARABBIA: "He don't sit with nobody."

TRAFICANT: "He don't sit with Jimmy ?"

(Apparently, Traficant was referring to Jimmy Prato.)

ORLIE CARABBIA: "He goes by the book, Jimmy."

Traficant also told the Carabbia brothers that he had laundered $10,000 of the Cleveland mob's money through the law firm of Ed Flask.

TRAFICANT: "Don't forget now. . . I had taken $10,000 down to Flask."

ORLIE CARABBIA: "For what?"

TRAFICANT: "Ten of our thousand down to Flask for him to give me some checks to cover up some of my contributions."

The next day, Charlie Carabbia returned to Prato and told him that Traficant refused the money, and said that he would not work with Prato and Naples, but would limit any deals to the Carabbias. Prato sent Carabbia back telling him not to take no for an answer. Reportedly, Carabbia never took the money back to Prato and Naples, and it was their understanding that the pay-off had been made. (Traficant would later explain that he accepted the mob money as part of a sting operation against Mahoning County racketeers.)

Though he had little more than a clean-cut image going for him, James Traficant beat the local democratic machine and took office. He promised to clean things up, and his vigorous performance was well covered by the media. Traficant targeted drug dealers and conducted many raids.

"We're gonna come down and knock your house apart. We're gonna find that lab," he declared. "I'm gonna notify every law enforcement agency in the states surrounding Ohio."

He planned to clean up the Youngstown suburb of Campbell, well-known for its gambling.

"I'm gonna say one thing to Campbell. Campbell has become known as the gambler's town. Campbell is a very good town, an excellent town, and most people don't like what goes on there. And if

Campbell doesn't straighten its own ship out, Campbell's gonna be in for a lot of hell from the sheriff's department."

And indeed, Sheriff Traficant did raise some hell in Campbell, arresting the mayor and charging him with running a gambling operation out of his grocery store. The charges against the mayor were dropped, but his sister and brother-in-law plead guilty.

In the 1970s, the Cleveland Mafia family gave control of the Youngstown vending and gambling rackets to Pittsburgh. In exchange, the Cleveland family received 25% of the profits from these operations. Youngstown and Pittsburgh received the rest. Angelo Lonardo met monthly with Jimmy Prato, Joey Naples or underboss Kelly Mannarino to pick up the Cleveland family's cut of the Youngstown profits. The profits averaged $5,000 or $6,000 monthly and on at least one occasion rose as high as $23,000.

During one of the meetings, in 1978, Prato and Naples told Lonardo that they were having problems with Charlie Carabbia. He would get drunk and bad-mouth Prato and Naples. Additionally, Prato and Naples suspected that Carabbia was lying about the number of poker machines he had in the Youngstown area.

Later at a Brown Derby restaurant, Prato and Naples met with Lonardo and Licavoli. This time they requested permission to kill Charlie Carabbia because they suspected Carabbia of stealing the bribe money that was supposed to go to then Sheriff-elect James Traficant.

Licavoli and Lonardo were opposed to killing Charlie Carabbia because of their respect for Ronnie Carabbia, who was in jail facing a murder charge in the bombing of Danny Greene. Additionally, Charlie was supporting Ronnie's family. Licavoli and Lonardo told Prato that they would talk to Charlie and resolve the problem.

A few days later, Lonardo and Licavoli met with Carabbia.

"Charlie, you're making a good living. Just mind your business and go along with Pittsburgh," Licavoli urged.

Three weeks later, Lonardo drove to Pittsburgh with Pat Feruccio. Feruccio, 61, was considered the video poker game expert for the Pittsburgh mob and their liaison to the Cleveland Mafia. Lonardo and Feruccio met with Pittsburgh Mafia boss John Larocca and underboss Gabriel "Kelly" Mannarino. Both LaRocca and Mannarino stated that they wanted Charlie Carabbia killed. Lonardo told them that he would talk to Charlie and clear up the problem.

"Charlie is taking care of Ronnie's family," Lonardo insisted.

"He did get rid of the Irishman for us," Licavoli added.

Perhaps Licavoli and Lonardo were worried about Ronnie Carabbia becoming a government witness against them in the Greene murder conspiracy if his brother was murdered. But Prato was adamant.

"If he continues to embarrass us and steal from us, we want him dead," he demanded in his thick Italian accent.

"If he doesn't stop, you do whatever you want," Licavoli replied.

On August 9, 1982, Sheriff James Traficant was arrested by the F.B.I. and charged with accepting bribes from organized crime figures, and filing a false income tax return for 1980. After the F.B.I. played the tapes that Charlie Carabbia secretly made, Traficant made a written confession. Traficant retained Carmen Policy to represent him. But when Traficant went live on local televsion with allegations of widespread corruption in the Mahoning Valley, Policy turned down the sheriff's case. In a surprise turn of events, Traficant recanted his confession and plead not guilty. The case went to U.S. District Court in Cleveland, with the feisty sheriff representing himself.

During the entertaining trial, Traficant defended himself well. He skillfully tore apart the government's case. He denied that he signed any confession and convinced the jury that he did not accept the money to join the mob, but was conducting his own sting operation. Traficant called Mahoning County the center of a vast network of cocaine trafficking. He said that several raids he recently directed had put a dent in those operations. During his closing argument, Traficant urged the jury to stand-fast and support him "like junkyard dogs in a hurricane."

The most astounding testimony came from one of Traficant's own deputies. Sergeant Joseph Hudak testified that Traficant asked him to shoot and wound him.

"The sheriff felt a shooting would help him counteract the federal government case. . .," Hudak stated. ". . .He said he would put his hand up and I should shoot him through the hand. . . He wanted to make it look like the Mob put a hit on him."

After four intense days of deliberations, the jurors sided with the former star high school football player and county drug counselor. They cited gaps in the tapes that could have been evidence of alteration. When the verdict was read, Traficant strode across the court room and began shaking hands with the jurors until the judge ordered him to stop.

The following day, Traficant returned home to Youngstown to a welcome fit for a hero. There was a victory party and reception at a church. Tee shirts adorned with the sheriff's portrait sold out quickly.

The one man who may have hurt Traficant's legal defense was Charlie Carabbia. And he was unavailable. His abandoned car had been found on the east side of Cleveland. A week later Lonardo and Licavoli met again with Prato and Naples.

"We heard Charlie was planning to clip us so we hit him," Prato revealed. "Sorry about the car Jack. Whoever drove didn't know where he was."

Lonardo spoke up. "Under no circumstances can we give our okay for Orlie to be hit. He's needed to care of Ronnie's family. And do us a favor Jimmy. Take $1,000 a month from our percentage and give it to Ronnie's wife."

Prato nodded in agreement.

◆   ◆   ◆

After his acquittal of the bribery charge, James Traficant was reelected to sheriff by an overwhelming majority. Anecdotes of his crime-fighting have been near-legendary and no doubt boosted the support he received when he ran for Congress in 1984 and was elected. He has maintained a special tie with the people of his district—hero status some would suggest.

Traficant began attracting attention in Congress after initiating his passionate and arm-flailing "one minutes," daily sixty-second sermons on a myriad of issues disturbing him. In fact he attracted so much attention with the one-minutes that television talk show host Phil Donahue devoted an entire hour to the Congressman.

Also bringing Traficant attention on Capitol Hill, is his appearance. With most politicians wearing expensive suits, Traficant has opted for aged, casual sport coats, leather boots and a loose tie all capped with his wispy, silver hair.

"I go to a local lawn and garden center and have it weed-whacked," Traficant jokes good-naturedly.

Likewise, Traficant's personal habits and outspokenness have brought him focus in Washington where he sleeps on an old, beat-up, wooden boat docked in a marina off Maine Avenue. He keeps a shotgun and pistol and warns, "if I catch somebody in my house at 2 o'clock in the morning, I wouldn't treat them like they were from the Welcome Wagon."

In Congress, Traficant has never pulled punches in expressing his dissatisfaction about American politics and feels that his one-minute presentations have helped.

"I'm sick and tired of this goddamed joint," he has complained. ". . .This place is a good old boy operation—people patting each other on the back and I don't get into that. I decided that if I started speaking out, maybe people would tune in and it would bring some change to Congress. . . This country is going bankrupt and we're listening to all these three-piece-suit Harvard graduates with their think-tank philosophies. . . Not that I'm some big shot. I'm just a jackass. I'm at the zenith of my jackass-hood. That's a fact. But my area is hurt. . . We're getting screwed. And I've come here for help."

Traficant has forced his point by attaching "Buy American" stipulations to most spending packages, and has actually succeeded in getting seven passed.

In 1987, Traficant was summoned back to court. This time he was facing civil charges by the I.R.S. for failing to pay taxes on the bribe money he received from Charlie Carabbia. The Congressman maintained that the money was accepted as campaign contributions, and was thus non-taxable. But he failed to report the funds on campaign finance reports. Traficant was confident.

"I'm going to fight the I.R.S. like a junkyard dog. . . I'll punch their lights out," he declared.

Again, the Carabbia tapes returned to haunt Traficant. His refusal to testify about them may have cost him his case. The Internal Revenue Service moved quickly to collect the back taxes and penalties. Traficant claimed his $96,000 salary was decreased to less than that of a first year teacher.

"There's no doubt about it," Traficant complained. "Government has stepped on me pretty good."

Chapter 49

Mafia boss James Licavoli didn't have long to celebrate his acquittal in the murder of Danny Greene. The Strike Force had prepared for the possibility of failure at the state level. Federal indictments for violation of the R.I.C.O. act were unsealed and he was arrested again in 1982, along with several mob associates.

"Danny Greene died five years ago and he's still fucking with us," a defense attorney scoffed.

Convicted of racketeering as a result of the federal charges were Licavoli, Ronnie Carabbia, John Calandra and ten, lower-level gangsters. U.S. District Court Judge William Thomas immediately revoked Licavoli's $400,000 bond.

"I am convinced you are the boss man of the enterprise to control criminal activity in northern Ohio," Thomas remarked. "I have to assume the enterprise is a going concern and you are getting income from it. . . It is not clear what has qualified you for Social Security in the past 10 years and why you have no known liabilities and don't know who pays your attorneys."

When the sentencing hearing came up, punishment was stiff. Licavoli was given 17 years and immediately shipped off to the Oxford, Wisconsin Correctional Institute. One of his prison-mates was Fast Eddie Watkins, the famous Ohio bank robber. Licavoli would later complain that the Wisconsin dampness aggravated his arthritis.

After numerous months on the F.B.I's top fugitive list, Tony Liberatore was finally arrested in Cleveland where he had been hiding at the home of a friend. He would be convicted of his role in bribing F.B.I. secretary Geraldine Rabinowitz and sentenced to 12 years.

Several months after the federal trials ended, Raymond Ferritto agreed to a paid interview for a Crime Inc. Mafia special which was to be aired on cable television's Discovery Channel. Following is an excerpt from the exchange.

> **INTERVIEWER:** How did you feel after you killed Greene? Were you elated?
>
> **FERRITTO:** . . . I was elated because the job was done and I was gonna become one of them and share in the profits. Something that since I was a kid, I dreamed of, I wanted. And this was my chance to do it.
>
> **INTERVIEWER:** Well how does it feel to kill someone that you know every living breath of because you're tapping his phone, you're living in the same building with him. What's it like to have a man as a target?
>
> **FERRITTO:** Well to me it was like having a glass of wine. It didn't mean a thing to me. I killed him and there was no remorse that I killed a man because that was part of my life. I was brought up all through my life believing that those, you just have to put them out of your mind, those were things, hurdles that you had to overcome. A man with a conscience doesn't last long on the street.

Despite a penalty of death for betraying omerta, Ferritto never showed any fear.

> **INTERVIEWER:** The Mafia has sworn to kill you. What is your comment?
>
> **FERRITTO:** I know that I am as capable of taking care of myself as the guy they send to take care of me. And it's just a matter of time for me. I'd be a fool to say that it isn't. Sooner or later they're gonna get me.

Chapter 50

In March of 1982, the Zagaria and Gallo multimillion dollar drug ring came to a halt when Carmen Zagaria was convicted in state court of selling drugs. He was sentenced to 10 to 30 years in prison but while free on bail, he became a fugitive. He lived out of state, secretly returning several times to see his family. On September 23rd, he returned to Cleveland, called the F.B.I. and told them to meet him at Holy Cross Cemetery. There, beside his mother's grave, Zagaria gave himself up. She had died while Zagaria was on the run, and he had not been able to come back to pay his respects.

During the time that Angelo Lonardo took over the Cleveland Mafia, law enforcers were closing in fast and hard on the Zagaria-Gallo drug operation. The haphazard killings, use of drugs by gang members, disorganization and lack of discipline aided the F.B.I.'s two-year investigation of the $15-million-a-year drug ring. The investigation utilized room bugs, phone taps and heavy surveillance.

Facing the original conviction and sentence, additional federal drug charges, weapons charges, and potential indictments against members of his family, Zagaria took the route that has become increasingly common in organized crime. He became a cooperating witness for the federal government.

With his near photographic memory, Zagaria would prove quite damaging to his former crime associates. His testimony would result in the indictments of Angelo Lonardo, Joey Gallo, Hans Graewe and Kevin McTaggart for vast narcotics dealings and almost one dozen murders.

In some of his debriefing, Zagaria cleared up the mystery surrounding the disappearance of several men including Danny Greene's former lieutenant, Keith Ritson. In April of 1978, Ritson and Hans Graewe had a falling out over a cocaine deal. Graewe believed that Ritson had cheated him. In August, an associate of Zagaria gave Ritson $2,500 to murder a drug dealer who had begun cooperating with police. Ritson had been drinking heavily and taking drugs. He kept the money but never committed the murder. Distrust and paranoia had become strong in the drug ring. When Zagaria approached him, Ritson revealed that he had several persons whom he wanted to kill, including his old buddy from Danny Greene's gang, Kevin McTaggart. Ritson's drug use continued to increase resulting in unstable behavior that Zagaria and Hans Graewe considered too much of a risk. For several months, they discussed killing him.

On November 16th, in the rear of Carmen Zagaria's fish store, he and Graewe sat with Ritson discussing drug business. Four workmen were doing odd jobs on the front exterior of the store.

I've gotta take a piss," Graewe said, getting up and walking away.

A few moments later, he returned quietly. In one quick motion Graewe placed a .38 revolver to the back of Ritson's head and pulled the trigger. Zagaria flinched as Ritson instantaneously collapsed in his seat. Zagaria was upset. He hadn't planned on killing Ritson in his store.

"I don't know why you did that, " he said rushing to look out into the front of the store. He didn't see the workmen.

Ritson's body shifted and dropped to the floor breaking one arm of the chair. Graewe slipped a kitty litter box under the head to catch the spurting blood.

"I don't know why you did that," Zagaria repeated. "I don't know if them guys heard you because they were out there working and all of a sudden they left. I don't know if anybody heard it."

Graewe's only response was to remove Ritson's watch, gold ring and necklace, and stuff them in his pocket. Zagaria's enforcers often stole jewelry off their victims, keeping them as trophies. Zagaria found Ritson's keys and placed them aside, then both men began cleaning up the blood. Graewe picked up a piece of clotted blood and stuck it on Zagaria's arm. Carmen recoiled in disgust and jerked his arm sending the red clump flying.

"You sick fuck! What did you do that for?" he demanded in anger.

The sadistic and morbid Graewe just laughed. They wrapped the body in a canvas sheet and secured it with wire. Graewe thought he saw slight movement in Ritson's body. He pulled out his revolver and fired one shot into the temple.

"Well, it looks like I'm back in the barbut game," he remarked casually referring to a dice game they had been running on the west side.

Zagaria drove Ritson's 1977 Lincoln to a department store. Graewe followed in his own van. The men parked the Lincoln and wiped it clean of fingerprints. Back at the fish store, they loaded Ritson's body into the van, drove it out to Jacquay Quarries where they wrapped it in plastic, secured it with heavy chain, and dumped it in a secluded pond.

Immediately after Zagaria flipped, he provided authorities with the location of Ritson's body and also that of Joe Giamo.

Police and U.S. Navy divers were sent out and eventually recovered both corpses.

Chapter 51

"Angelo Lonardo is probably one of the most respected guys in the whole United States. . . ," said mob lieutenant Joe Gallo one day. "He's really the kind of guy we needed in this town a long time ago, but you know, nobody ever listened to him because. . . he don't express himself. . . But out of everybody that's left, this guy commands a lot of respect. . .One thing I know is people, and he is a beautiful person. Besides that, he's my boss, you know but forget that, because I've had a lot of people that ain't worth the powder to blow them away..I respect him not only because I have to because, I'm telling you, he's a great guy."

The conversation, secretly recorded by the F.B.I., would come back to haunt the mob and Joe Gallo, in more ways than one.

Indeed Gallo was right. Lonardo was greatly respected nationally by many of the most powerful Mafia leaders. And his quiet nature, typical of the last breed of Mafiosi, was a form of protection against such treacherous betrayers of the brotherhood like Jimmy Fratianno.

Even police detectives and F.B.I. agents had a certain respect for Lonardo.

"To me, he was almost like the movie version of The Godfather," a policeman commented. "He was always the gentleman, not a tough street rat. He was someone who recognized us as people in the same general line of work—on an opposing team, of course."

And Lonardo maintained respect for the police. When detectives would arrive at his home to execute a search or arrest warrant, Lonardo and his wife would treat them like guests even inviting them to sit and have coffee.

Strike Force prosecutor Donna Congeni was impressed with Lonardo's demeanor in the court room. She was subjected to cruel, obscene insults from some of the other defendants and even their attorneys. But Lonardo treated her with respect and courtesy, even standing when she approached the defendant's table.

"He was the epitome of class," she once remarked.

But Congeni was just as determined to send Lonardo away for life as she was the others. The task proved challenging.

"Because of his years of careful training in the art of secrecy and insulation, with meetings held in back rooms and decisions made with nods and coded phrases, our case against Angelo Lonardo was difficult to prove," said prosecutor Congeni. "But once informant Carmen Zagaria testified about Lonardo's methods, the jury could see his power and control."

As a result of sentences handed down by U.S. District Court Judge John Manos, Kevin McTaggart, Hans Graewe, Joey Gallo and, Angelo Lonardo would be destined to life behind federal bars. In a separate trial, Tommy Sinito pleaded guilty and was sentenced to 22 years in prison.

It had been a career proving crime pays. For decades, Big Ange Lonardo survived the most hazardous pitfalls of Mafia involvement— mob bullets and prison. Through fifty years of acquiring power and money through criminal and legitimate enterprises, he had spent only eighteen months incarcerated. It was the boldly executed vendetta to avenge the untimely loss of his father that resulted in that loss of freedom and launched his life in La Cosa Nostra.

F.B.I. agents had been visiting Lonardo and offering deals since his conviction in 1983. They promised to get him out of prison on an appeal bond. No doubt it was a tough decision. The mob sentence for violating omerta is death and the despicable label of "rat."

In August of 1983, Lonardo was brought to Kansas City to testify before the U.S. grand jury investigating skimming from several Las Vegas casinos. Lonardo refused to address questions alleging that he transported skimming proceeds between Chicago and Cleveland. Despite an offer of immunity and a judicial order, he would not betray omerta.

But back in his lonely cell at Lewisburg Prison, Lonardo must have been weighing his options. Perhaps life away from his family, his Cadillac and beautiful house were too much to give up. It was only after his first judicial appeal was denied that he picked up the F.B.I. agent's business card and quietly slipped away to a prison pay phone. He had made a painfully tormenting decision that would have far-reaching effects throughout the national underworld.

"Are you still there?" he quietly asked.

Indeed the F.B.I. agent knew what Lonardo meant. He was swiftly removed from Lewisburg, placed under 24 hour guard and the long process of betraying his past began.

When the word spread, Lonardo's relatives and friends couldn't believe it. They were shocked. If Danny Greene was watching, no doubt he was beaming at the chaos his war with La Cosa Nostra had sparked.

In the underworld, gangsters from New York to Los Angeles were reflecting on past dealings with Lonardo, nervously wondering what he might reveal. Fifty years of high-level Mafia knowledge was surely going to hurt a lot of people. It started with someone once very close to Lonardo. Several days before Lonardo's defection was made public, 81-year-old Jack Licavoli was removed from Oxford Correctional Institute and admitted to a local hospital. He had suffered a heart attack and would die five days later. Licavoli had been a quiet and common prisoner.

"Nothing fazed him," his attorney Jim Willis commented. "Some people just don't cry. He was one of those people who did not cry."

Angelo Lonardo's defection was a grand prize—a coup for the F.B.I. Joseph Griffin, then agent-in-charge of the F.B.I. field office in Cleveland must have been delighted.

"Jimmy Fratianno was a captain. Joseph Valachi was a mere soldier," he explained to the news media. "Lonardo is to Fratianno and Valachi what the president of General Motors is to a foreman and an assembly line worker."

They've been referred to as rats, stool pigeons or stoolies. Mobsters hate them and the Justice Department loves them. After weeks of debriefing, legal procedures and judicial technicalities, Angelo Lonardo, known appropriately in F.B.I. files as "Top Notch," was ready.

The first stop was back to Kansas City where prosecutors had been unhindered by Lonardo's previous refusal to talk. They had returned indictments and the historic Strawman II skimming trial was underway. Among the defendants was Angelo's once-dear brother-in-law and companion Maishe Rockman.

Seated in the witness chair, seventy-four-year-old Lonardo looked aged and weary. But his testimony was effective. In addition to Rockman, numerous mobsters were convicted of skimming more than $2 million from two Las Vegas casinos. They included:

Joseph Aiuppa, 78, boss of the Chicago Mafia
John "Jackie" Cerone, 71, Chicago underboss
Joseph Lombardo, 57, Chicago capo
Angelo "The Hook" LaPietra, Chicago capo
Frank Balistrieri, Milwaukee mob boss (plead guilty)
Carl DeLuna, Kansas City underboss (plead guilty)

Following the trial, Jimmy Fratianno was used as an F.B.I. witness during the detention hearings. He provided key testimony used to incarcerate Aiuppa and the others without bail pending sentencing. Fratianno also testified that it was Aiuppa who ordered the murder of west coast mob boss Johnny Roselli in 1976.

Lonardo spent the next three years in other federal court rooms and before the U.S. Senate Permanent Subcommittee on Investigations revealing everything he knew about the mob's operations. During one exchange with Senator Sam Nunn, he instructed the committee on the difference between a gang and a Mafia family.

SENATOR NUNN: You mention the murder of Leo Moceri. Who committed that murder?

LONARDO: I believe it was Danny Greene and Keith Ritson.

SENATOR NUNN: Why was that murder committed?

LONARDO: Well, Leo Moceri and John Nardi did not get along, and one day during the feast that they hold in Cleveland every year, in Mayfield—I think you know about that—Leo Moceri told John Nardi to mind his own business and he had better start behaving or otherwise he was going to get it. He says, "You know I'm the underboss now, he says, "don't forget."

SENATOR NUNN: How was that murder carried out?

LONARDO: Well. John Nardi was being tried in Miami on narcotics and while he was there he gave Danny Greene the order,
the contract to try to get Leo Moceri.

SENATOR NUNN: Was that murder carried out by the other
gang, another gang -

LONARDO: Yes

SENATOR NUNN [continuing]. Against a member of your gang?

LONARDO: Against a member of our gang? No. He was a member of our family.

SENATOR NUNN: And someone from another family carried
out the contract on him?

LONARDO: It was not a family. It was Danny Greene and Keith
Ritson.

SENATOR NUNN: Did they belong to any kind of family at all?
Was there any kind of -

LONARDO: They were what you call a gang.

Lonardo's knowledge of the underworld was brought from the Las
Vegas skimming trial in Kansas City to New York City. There in
September of 1986, he and Jimmy Fratianno were key witnesses at the
United States vs. Salerno trial. Dubbed the "commission case," this
highly publicized and successful attack on organized crime began in
1980, when the New York City F.B.I. initiated an ambitious assault on
the Mafia.

Strike Force teams were assigned to build R.I.C.O. cases against
each of the five Mafia clans in New York. The operation included
New York State Organized Crime Task Force investigators, N.Y.P.D.
detectives and U.S. attorneys. Six years of investigation were capped
by indictments of numerous high-ranking mobsters, including the
bosses who make up the elite Mafia ruling commission. The case was
dubbed "Star Chamber" by the investigators. In all, there were 37
counts of loansharking, labor payoffs, extortion and racketeering.

In addition to Clevelanders Angelo Lonardo and Jimmy Fratianno,
the prosecution also had celebrated F.B.I. agent, Joseph Pistone on
their side. Under the assumed name of Donnie Brasco, Pistone had
gone undercover and infiltrated the Bonnano crime family. His historic
penetration of La Cosa Nostra's inner circle netted a wealth of invalu-

able intelligence which provided an in-depth look at the structure and operations of New York City's five Mafia families. Pistone told his story in the book *Donnie Brasco—my undercover life in the Mafia.*
All of the commission case defendants were convicted and sentenced as follows:

Anthony "Fat Tony" Salerno (Genovese family boss) 100 years; $240,000 fine

Aniello "Neil" Dellacroce (Gambino family underboss) 100 years; $240,000 fine

Carmine "Junior the Snake" Persico (Colombo family boss) 100 years; $240,000 fine

Gennaro "Gerry Lang" Langella (Colombo family underboss) 100 years; $240,000 fine

Ralph Scopo (Colombo soldier) 100 years; $240,000 fine

Anthony "Tony Ducks" Corallo (Lucchese family boss) 100 years; $250,000 fine

Salvatore "Tommy Mix" Santoro (Luchesse family underboss) 100 years; $250,000 fine

Christopher "Christy Tick" Furnari (Luchesse family consigliere) 100 years; $240,000 fine

Gambino family boss, Paul Castellano, had also been indicted, but prior to the trial was killed in a plot led by his cocky lieutenant, John Gotti. Gotti took over the Gambino family after Castellano's murder. Dubbed "Dapper Don" because of his impeccable appearance and "Teflon Don" because of his numerous acquittals, Gotti eventually received a life sentence for the Castellano conspiracy.

In the meantime, the Justice Department had decided to remove Jimmy Fratianno from the WITSEC payroll after ten years of service. During his tenure as a federal cooperating witness, Fratianno commissioned author Ovid Demaris to write his biography entitled *The Last Mafioso*, and co-authored another book—*Vengeance is Mine*—with journalist Michael Zuckerman. Later Fratianno sued Demaris claiming that the book contained false quotes. He blamed the criticism of WITSEC in *Vengeance is Mine* for his being dropped from the witness protection program.

The Justice Department said it had spent $1 million protecting Fratianno—a figure that Jimmy disputed. A spokesman said that any further payments would make WITSEC look like a pension fund for aging mobsters. It was agreed though that Fratianno would continue to receive protection in danger areas.

Jimmy was still bitter. "They just threw me out on the street," he complained. "I put 30 guys away, six of them bosses, and now the whole world's looking for me."

Despite the Mafia contract on his life, his removal from WITSEC and several appearances on national talk shows, Fratianno was able to live another six years until his natural death in 1993. He was 79.

Chapter 52

Peanuts Tronolone had been the Cleveland Mafia's figurehead boss ever since Angelo Lonardo turned government witness. He was a mobster in the same generation as James Licavoli. Though Peanuts didn't have a fortune like Licavoli had amassed before he died, he was every bit as treacherous.

John Tronolone was born in 1910 in Buffalo, New York, where his father owned a laundry. As a teenager, John used to hand out peanuts to the children of his father's customers, earning him the name "Peanuts." Tronolone's first arrest was at age 15 for gambling. By age 21, he had four gambling arrests and a burglary charge on his record. He served nine months in prison for possessing criminal tools. Originally an associate member of the Buffalo Mafia, Peanuts was made into the Cleveland La Cosa Nostra in the forties.

In the mid-forties Peanuts left Cleveland for the open gambling territory of Miami, where many elected officials encouraged the loose enforcement of gambling laws to promote tourism. In Miami Beach, Tronolone bought into the Tahiti Club, which became a hangout for racketeers heading south for sun and sin. Later he opened a travel agency.

By the sixties, Tronolone had become well known in mob circles for running a sports-betting operation in southern Florida. Top mobsters like Angelo Lonardo and James Licavoli visited him whenever they went south to escape the bitter Cleveland winters. Tronolone became very close with Tony Salerno, an up-and-coming power in New York's Genovese Crime Family which represented the Cleveland family on the national Mafia ruling commission. Peanuts was known to joke that he considered himself a member of both the Cleveland Mafia and the Genovese family.

In 1975, Tronolone was convicted of running a $1-million-a-week bookmaking operation. He was sentenced to two years in prison and fined $2,000.

◆   ◆   ◆

On March 21, 1980, Angelo Bruno, boss of the Philadelphia Mafia, was seated in a car when someone placed a double-barrel shotgun to the back of his head and pulled both triggers. Bruno's murder touched off a vicious mob war resulting in fifteen murders.

As a result, Philadelphia mob capo John "Johnny Keys" Simone was sentenced to death by the Gambino family. Simone sought the help of John Tronolone, whom he had known for some time. He flew to Florida and begged Tronolone to speak with Tony Salerno and straighten out things with the commission. Tronolone agreed and had Simone pay for his trip to New York. But Peanuts had no intention of seeking mercy for Simone. Tronolone's loyalty was to the Genovese family. On a short trip to New York, Tronolone spoke with Salerno and told him that he would send Simone to New York.

"I'll get him there, then you guys can do whatever you want with him," Peanuts offered.

When Tronolone returned to Florida, he contacted Simone and told him that Salerno was patching things up with Gambino boss Paul Castellano. Tronolone sold Simone a plane ticket. In the meantime, Castellano had assigned capo Sammy "the Bull" Gravano to murder Simone.

As a ruse to get close to his target, Gravano told Simone that the Gambino family was supporting him to take over the Philadelphia La Cosa Nostra. Simone was excited but cautious, and began meeting with Gravano.

On September 17, 1980, Simone had his last meeting with Gravano. Sammy the Bull and a team of his mob crew members forced Simone into a van and drove him to a secluded area.

". . . Joey went to grab him and pull him out," Gravano later recalled in his biography Underboss. "He kicked out at Joey right in the chest. [Johnny] said, 'I'll walk out on my own. Let me die like a man.' He took five or six steps. Without a word,

he lowered his head, quiet and dignified. I nodded at Louie Milito. As requested by Johnny Keys, he would be killed by a made member. Louie put a .357 magnum to the back of Johnny's head and fired. The shot immediately leveled him to the ground. He died instantly. . ."

"*I had to tell Paul [Castellano] that I was literally sick about this,*" *Gravano would say. "We had just killed a guy who was the epitome, in my opinion, of our life, everything we were supposed to be. . . This is one hit I'm never going to be proud of. . ."*

◆   ◆   ◆

During several weeks in the spring of 1989, Peanuts Tronolone had been talking with an ex-Hell's Angel named Jack Roper, who owned a string of massage parlors in Florida. Roper said he had $1.7 million in stolen diamonds which had been smuggled in from Europe. Anxious at the opportunity to make a profitable deal, Tronolone agreed to meet Roper who was going to hand over $15,000 worth of the stolen gems to settle a friend's gambling debt. If Peanuts liked the diamonds, then he would help fence the rest through his Mafia contacts.

On a sunny morning in April, Peanuts eased his 1987 Toyota in the parking lot of a diner near the race track in Hallandale. He was excited about meeting Roper and it was only a few minutes when the biker walked up to Tronolone's car door. Roper was a large, fierce looking man with a long beard, a jean jacket with cut off sleeves, sunglasses and a bandana tied around his head. Roper introduced himself and the men shook hands. Roper dropped a small cloth bag sealed with a twist tie in Tronolone's lap.

"See if you like them. I think you'll love them," Roper said.

"Oh I don't want to look at them here," Peanuts said as he untwisted the tie to get a peek inside the bag.

"You want to go and have coffee or what?" Tronolone suggested.

"Aw naw," Roper replied while motioning with his hand as Peanuts looked at the diamonds.

It was such tunnel vision and temporary loss of street sense that had befallen so many other mobsters. Despite a lifetime of crime,

Peanuts failed to recognize that Roper was a fake. Suddenly four plainclothes investigators from the Broward County Sheriff's Department swooped in—their guns leveled at the Cleveland don.

"John Tronolone, you're under arrest," announced Roper, in reality Lt. David Green, officer in charge of Broward's organized crime squad.

Prosecutors and federal agents nationwide would applaud the collar in disbelief. Never before had a Mafia family boss been caught red-handed in a direct transfer of contraband. Peanuts would be labeled a bumbler not even wise enough to employ an underling to handle the risky street operations of such a deal.

In the months to come, Peanuts Tronolone, the absentee landlord and figurehead of the Cleveland Mafia would be convicted of racketeering, loan-sharking and dealing in stolen property. After the fallout from the Danny Greene murder, it would be the government's coup de grace, all but officially ending the seven-decade life of the once-mighty Cleveland Mafia.

Problems only continued for the Cleveland underworld. In 2001, it was revealed that Anthony P. Delmonti, a low-level mob associate had been working as an informant for the F.B.I. for several years. Delmonti's information would contribute to the indictment of Cleveland's longtime gambling figure Virgil Ogletree, 1960's partner of Don King, who was reputed to be running a large numbers operation. Delmonti's knowledge stretched to Rochester, New York where his former attorney would be indicted on drug-related charges.

# Chapter 53

On June 3, 1996, Ernie Biondillo, an organized crime figure, was driving on the east side of Youngstown when he was boxed in by two carloads of black males wearing walkie-talkie headsets. Two of the men ran up to Biondillo's Cadillac and sprayed the car with ten shotgun blasts. According to the F.B.I., Biondillo's murder resulted from his encroaching on the territory of Lenine "Lenny" Strollo.

After Jimmy Prato died in 1981, Joey Naples became the Pittsburgh overlord of the Youngstown's rackets. In 1987, he and Lenny Strollo were reportedly made into the Pittsburgh La Cosa Nostra. Strollo, a nephew of Prato, was given a significant portion of the Mahoning Valley rackets to oversee and was permitted to operate independently of Naples. Both Naples and Strollo had their own sets of loyalists and mistrust between the two factions began to fester. In 1990, Strollo was convicted of bribing two police officers and racketeering in connection with several gambling operations, including an elaborate Campbell, Ohio casino known as the All-American Club or Bernie's. Strollo was sentenced to fourteen months. Strollo feared Naples would take over his gambling operations when he went to prison, an F.B.I. informant revealed.

In August of 1991, Joey Naples was surveying his mansion-size house being built in Beaver Township in southern Mahoning County. Several shots rang out and Naples fell dead. The sniper had concealed himself in a cornfield across the street. After Naples' murder, Lenny Strollo became the Pittsburgh Mafia representative in the Mahoning Valley. He has numerous mob associates under his supervision. Among them are Bernard "Bernie the Jew" Altshuler and Lawrence "Jeep" Garono. Strollo reported to Henry "Zebo" Zottola, a high-ranking member of the Pittsburgh La Cosa Nostra.

In 1996, Ernie Biondillo, a former Naples associate, tried taking over part of Strollo's operation. Biondillo had placed poker machines in private clubs in Hillsville, Pennsylvania, an area considered Strollo territory. He also paid off politicians without informing Strollo.

Information provided to the F.B.I. revealed that Bernie Altshuler engineered the murder of Biondillo and that four black drug dealers were paid $35,000 to carry out the hit. One of the hitmen plead guilty to a federal charge of committing murder to further a racketeering enterprise. He awaits sentencing while another of the killers was recently arrested on the same charge.

Another major investigation centered around the Mahoning Valley Sanitary District and fired board member Ed Flask. The politically-connected Flask was suspected in the embezzlement of $1.9 million. He would eventually plead guilty to several charges and admit that he used his position to collect over $1-million from firms doing business with the district. It was through the law office of Flask, that former sheriff James Traficant was recorded telling Charlie Carabbia that he had laundered $10,000 in Mafia bribe money.

The sanitary district scandal and Biondillo's murder have occurred amidst an intensive and continuing F.B.I. investigation into organized crime and political corruption in the Youngstown area, the unsolved killing of Joey Naples, and the most disturbing attempted murder of Mahoning County Prosecutor Paul Gains. The probe has utilized Title III wiretaps on cellular telephones, informants and cooperating witnesses. The cooperating witnesses have been most effective and have become more readily available. Over the years, swapping testimony for leniency has become commonplace in the underworld.

"There's a substantial opportunity to have a definite impact on the organized crime problem in Youngstown and the Mahoning Valley," F.B.I. Agent Van Harp said in 1997.

That impact might very well reach all the way to the nation's capital. Part of the Mahoning Valley investigation has focused on alleged corrupt activities by Congressman James Traficant. The feisty, controversial representative himself stated to the media, in 2000, that he expects to be indicted.

Epilogue

"It is very ironic," said F.B.I. agent Joe Griffin. "During his life, Danny Greene always tried to take out the Cleveland La Cosa Nostra. He was never able to do it. In his death, he did."

Consider that as a result of Raymond Ferritto flipping, Jimmy Fratianno became a prized cooperating witness for the Federal Bureau of Investigation. Together, his and Ferritto's testimony dismantled most of the Cleveland La Cosa Nostra hierarchy. To regain their power and money, the Cleveland mob became involved in drugs and as a result, underboss Angelo Lonardo was sentenced to life in prison. He flipped and at the time, was the highest ranking mobster ever to betray omerta. The testimony of he and Fratianno was used across the country in unprecedented convictions of major La Cosa Nostra family bosses, which resulted in the fall of the Kansas City, Milwaukee and Cleveland Mafia families.

Once it was apparent that the Unitied States government could protect major Mafia witnesses like Fratianno and Lonardo, the option of trading information for freedom appeared more attractive to gangsters caught in the F.B.I.'s mob dragnet. Consider the Fiato Brothers whose testimony and that of Fratianno was instrumental in the F.B.I.'s attack on the Southern California Mafia family. Other ranking mob figures followed the lead including Luchesse soldier Henry Hill, Vincent "Fish" Cafaro, right-hand man to Genovese boss Tony Salerno, and Philadelphia Mafia underboss Phil Leonetti. The most recent celebrated La Cosa Nostra turncoat was Gotti underboss, Sammy "the Bull" Gravano.

Indeed, Danny Greene's most important legacy was left in his death. It was a death that sparked the events leading to a parade of La

Cosa Nostra defectors, whose secrets would be crucial to the government's success in the war against the Mafia. Danny would have been proud.

Some day he'll die, as all we must, some will laugh but most will cry. His legend will live on for years, to bring his friends mixed pleasure. (From The Ballad of Danny Greene)

What Happened to Them?

Frank Balistrieri head of the Milwaukee La Cosa Nostra died of natural causes in 1993. He was 74.

Frank Brancato partner in the Licatese faction of the Cleveland Mafia, was 76 when he died of natural causes in 1973.

Elmer Brittain associate of the Celtic Club, was killed in January of 1977. His murder is officially unsolved.

Dominic P. Brooklier Southern California Mafia boss died in prison in 1984. He was 71 and had heart problems.

Allie Calabrese died in prison in 1999 while serving a sentence for attempting to defraud a New Jersey bank.

John Calandra Jack Licavoli's right-hand man, died of natural causes in 1992.

Ronnie Carabbia Youngstown mobster convicted of killing Danny Greene, served almost 23 years in prison before being paroled in 2002.

Eugene "the Animal" Ciasullo now in his sixties and semi-retired, is perhaps the most successful of modern-day Cleveland La Cosa Nostra figures. He has maintained a widely respected reputation nationwide, while managing to serve minimal time in prison. He did spend two years in prison for a 1981 assault conviction. Ciasullo has two residences in Pennsylvania, and spends winters at a third in Florida.

Pasquale "Butchie" Cisternino died in prison in 1990 of pancreatic cancer. He was 56 and left behind a wife and six children.

Morris "Moe" Dalitz died in 1989 at the age of 89. By then he was ironically known in the legitimate community as the "godfather of Las Vegas" and his worth was estimated at $110 million. Much of his success was due to the legitimate investments he made with his money from rumrunning and gambling. His obituaries, which highlighted his career of crime were undoubtedly a revelation to many who were unaware of his background.

John DeMarco boss of the Licatese faction of the Cleveland La Cosa Nostra, died of a heart attack in 1972, at the age of 68. In his later years, he confined his mob activities to lending money on a short-term, high-interest basis.

Raymond Ferritto left WITSEC after only one year lived in Pennsylvania. In 1992, he was convicted of criminal conspiracy and bookmaking charges. He served a short prison stint, was given three years probation and ordered to pay $10,500 in fines. He retired to Florida in 2000 and died of congestive heart failure in 2004.

Pasquale "Pat" Feruccio was sentenced in 1997 to two years in prison for violating his parole by associating with known felons and for conspiring to obstruct the National Indian Gaming Commission. He and a Pittsburgh Mafia associate reportedly had hidden interests in a company that bribed a tribal councilman to finance and manage a casino on the Rincon Indian Reservation near San Diego, California. Feruccio lived quietly in Canton, Ohio, still semi-active in several legitimate businesses until his death in 2006 at the age of 88.

Jimmy "the Weasel" Fratianno died of Alzheimer's disease and a stroke in 1985. He was 79.

Joey Gallo once heir apparent to the Cleveland Mafia throne, continues to serve a life sentence for drug racketeering.

Michael Genovese boss of the Pittsburgh Mafia, is believed to be retired or semi-retired and living in Florida.

Hartmut "the Surgeon" Graewe the sadistic and vicious drug ring enforcer continues to serve a life sentence.

Joseph "Joe Loose" Iacobacci an acknowledged member of La Cosa Nostra has had continued involvement in organized crime. In 1996 he was sentenced to thirty months for his federal conviction in a scheme to defraud $3-million from several New Jersey banks. He has also served time for gambling and drug convictions. Iacobacci was released from his most recent prison sentence in 1998. Some consider "Loose" the current boss of the Cleveland mob.

John LaRocca longtime boss of the Pittsburgh La Cosa Nostra, died in 1984. He was 83.

Tony Liberatore who was able to penetrate the security of the Cleveland F.B.I. and steal a secret list of confidential informants was once called heir to the Cleveland mob throne. He was released from prison in 1990 after serving eight years for racketeering. In 1993 he was convicted of money laundering and racketeering and sentenced to ten years. The conviction was upheld by the U.S. Supreme Court in 1995. Liberatore had appealed on the grounds that he suffered from Alzheimer's Disease and thus was incompetent to stand trial. He died in prison in 1998.

James "Jack White" Licavoli died in prison in 1985. He was 81.

Angelo "Big Ange" Lonardo was dropped from WITSEC around 1991 after moving back to northeast Ohio, an area obviously forbidden by the program. He lived quietly until his death in 2006 at the age of 95.

Gabriel "Kelly" Mannarino died of natural causes in 1981.

Kevin McTaggart continues to serve a life sentence at the federal penitentiary in Terre Haute, Indiana. He is secretary of a Jaycees group made up of inmates. In 1989, he received a commendation for rushing to the aid of a female prison psychologist who had been stabbed by a disturbed inmate.

Anthony "the Old Man" Milano died in 1978 of natural causes. He was 90.

Frank Milano died of natural causes in the sixties.

John "Curly" Montana was linked to the 1981 killing of bar owner Stanley Lentzas. At the request of a prominent businessman, Montana took on the murder contract but first sought the permission of Angelo Lonardo to handle such a hit outside the family concerns. After the contract was carried out, Montana offered Lonardo some of the money he had received for the murder. Montana was never charged in that murder or in the killing of John Nardi. However he did serve 13 years in prison for his involvement in the 1981 kidnapping and murder of Chicago millionaire businessman Henry Podborny. In 2001, Montana, age 82 was investigated for trying to sell a stolen painting worth $700,000. He was not charged and continues to reside in Cleveland.

Jimmy Prato Youngstown mob boss, died of a heart attack in 1988. He was 81.

Jackie Presser died of lung cancer in 1988 at the age of 62.

Maishe Rockman was released from prison in 1993, for health reasons, after serving seven years of a twenty-one year sentence imposed from his skimming case conviction. He died in 1995.

Tommy Sinito died of a heart attack in prison in 1997. He was 59. He was serving several concurrent sentences, including a seven-to-25 year stint for the murder of mob associate and bodyguard David Perrier. Sinito's former attorney, Jim Willis, called him an honorable friend. "If he told you something, you could take it to the bank," Willis said. "He wasn't a crybaby like they put in jail today, calling you every five minutes collect, complaining about their sentence. He was from the old school."

Lenine "Lenny" Strollo continues to be a primary target of an aggressive F.B.I. attack on organized crime in Ohio's Mahoning Valley.

Babe Triscaro died of a stroke in 1974.

John "Peanuts" Tronolone died of heart problems in 1991. He was 80.

Ernest "Ted" Waite associate of Danny Greene from the firechasing business, disappeared in April of 1980. Police found bullet casings, a pool of blood and a formula to refine cocaine at his house. The murder is officially unsolved.

Carmen Zagaria is out of WITSEC and living comfortably in an undisclosed location. He reportedly visits relatives in Cleveland on occasion.

Sources

BOOKS

Allen, Edward J. *Merchants of Menace—The Mafia*. Charles C. Thomas 1962

Anastasia, George. *Mob Father*. Zebra Books 1993

Delaney, Frank. *The Celts*. Little, Brown and Co. 1986.

Demaris, Ovid. *The Last Mafioso*. Times Books 1981.

Ehle, Jay C. *Cleveland's Harbor*. The Kent State University Press 1996.

Fox, Stephen. *Blood and Power*. Penguin Books 1989.

Giancana, Sam and Chuck. *Double Cross*. Warner Books 1992.

Jacobs, James B. with Christopher Panarella and Jay Worthington. *Busting the Mob*. New York University Press 1994.

Kobler, John. *Capone*. G.P. Putnam's Sons 1971.

Lavigne, Yves. *Hell's Angels*. Lyle Stuart/Carole Publishing Group 1996.

Maas, Peter. *The Valachi Papers*. G.P. Putnam's Sons 1968.

Maas, Peter. *Underboss*. HarperCollins 1997

Messick, Hank and Goldblatt, Burt. *The Mobs and the Mafia*. Ballantine Books, Inc. 1972

Messick, Hank. *The Silent Syndicate*. Macmillan Co. 1967.

Neff, James. *Mobbed Up*. Bantam Doubleday Dell Publishing Group, Inc. 1989.

New American Bible, (St. Joseph Edition) Catholic Book Publishing Co. 1970.

Newfield, Jack. *Only in America*. William Morrow and Co. 1995.

Place, Robin. *The Celts (Peoples of the Past)*. MacDonald Educational Limited 1977.

Porrello, Rick. *The Rise and Fall of the Cleveland Mafia*. Barricade Books 1995.

Ressler, Robert K. and Shachtman, Tom. *Justice is Served* St. Martin's Press 1994.

Roemer, William F. Jr. *The Enforcer*. Ballantine Books 1994.

Van Tassel, David D. and Grabowski, John. J., editors. *The Encyclopedia of Cleveland History*. Indiana University Press. 1987.

Zuckerman, Michael. *Vengeance is Mine*. Macmillan Co. 1987

MAGAZINE/NEWSPAPER ARTICLES

Aikens, Tom and Gazarick, Richard and Erdley, Debra. Three-part series on the lives of the late Samuel and Gabriel "Kelly" Mannarino, *Tribune-Review*, June 2-4, 1996

Cleveland Magazine, "Come Home, Jack White," *Cleveland Magazine* (Inside Cleveland), Dec. 1984

Congressional Quarterly, "Traficant Owes Back Taxes; Konnyu in Trouble at Home," *Inside Congress*, Sep. 19, 1987

Drexler, Michael. "Default. The Real Story," *Cleveland Edition*, Dec. 15, 1988.

Kobler, John. "Crime Town U.S.A.," *Saturday Evening Post*, March 9, 1963

Inland Seas Magazine "Cleveland as a World Port" Fall, 1948

Maas, Peter. "Who is the Mob Today," *Parade Magazine—Akron Beacon Journal*, Feb. 25, 1996

Magnuson, Ed. "Headhunters," Time Magazine, December 1, 1986.

Marshall, Samuel F. Probe of Daniel Greene and Local 1317 of the International Longshoremens Association. *Cleveland Plain Dealer*, Sep. 13, 1964—Sep. 26, 1964

Murphy, Kim. "2 'Made Guys' Took Only Way Out—Inform for FBI," *Los Angeles Times*, April 16, 1988.

Murphy, Kim "The Godfather's Son," *Los Angeles Times*, Sep. 17, 1989.

Neff, James. "Can the Mafia Make a Comeback?" *Cleveland Magazine*, August, 1989.

Neff, James. "How the Mob Edited Your Morning Newspaper," *Cleveland Magazine*, November, 1989

O'Donnell, Doris. "Theatrical Grill," *The Times of Your Life*, Holiday Issue, 1995.

Robb, David. "Hollywood Heavy," *L.A. Weekly*, July 7-13, 1995.

Roberts, Michael D. "Why They Blew Shondor Birns Away," *Cleveland Magazine*, Date Unkown

Roberts, Michael D. "Public Enemy Shondor Birns," *Cleveland Magazine*, November 1990

Romano, Lois. "Jim Traficant, Wild Man On the Hill," Washington Post, April 23, 1990.

Rowan, Roy. "The Biggest Mafia Bosses," *Fortune*, Nov. 10, 1986.

Sciria, Paul. "Babe," *La Gazetta Italiana*, May 1995.

Sheridan, Terence. "The Death of Shondor Birns and the Rise of Danny Greene," *Exit Magazine*. July 16, 1975.

Sheridan, Terence. "High Life," *Cleveland Magazine*, August, 1988.

Trebilcock, Bob. "Mean Streets," *Ohio Magazine*, January, 1980.

Whelen, Edward P. "The Life and Hard Times of Cleveland's Mafia-How the Danny Greene Murder Exploded the Godfather Myth," *Cleveland Magazine*, August 1978.

Whelen, Edward P. "The Lonardo Papers," *Cleveland Magazine*, December, 1985.

Wolf, Richard. "Ohio lawmaker takes to TV," USA Today, March, 1990

NEWSPAPERS
Akron Beacon Journal
Cincinnati Post
Cleveland Press
Cleveland Plain Dealer
Lake County News Herald
Los Angeles Times
New York Times
Pittsburgh Post-Gazette
Pittsburgh Press
Sun Newspapers
The Sunday Paper (Lake-Geauga)
Warren Tribune Chronicle
Washington Post
Youngstown Vindicator

CABLE TELEVISION
The Discovery Channel: Crime Inc. The Cleveland Mafia

FEDERAL GOVERNMENT DOCUMENTS
Organized Crime Strike Force file on the Danny Greene murder conspiracy

Federal Bureau of Investigation files:
Field Office file 92-2748 and Bureau file 183-1331 (Danny Greene murder conspiracy)
F.B.I affidavit of S.A. Michael Kahoe 3-78
F.B.I. affidavit of S.A. Thomas Kirk 3-78
F.B.I. affidavit of S.A. Robert Friedrick 11-77
F.B.I. affidavit of S.A. Michael Kahoe 12-77
F.B.I. affidavit of S.A. Robert Friedrick 10-77
F.B.I. affidavit of S.A. George Grotz 1977
F.B.I. intercepted conversations from the residence of James Licavoli pursuant to court-ordered Title III wiretap surveillance 1977.
Frank Milano File—F.O.I.P.A. request file number 92-3229

Drug Enforcement Administration files
Shondor Birns
Daniel J. Greene
Keith Ritson

United States Senate Permanent Subcommittee on Investigations of the Committee on Governmental Affairs:
Profile of Organized Crime: Great Lakes Region, Jan. 25-31, 1984 (Testimony of Peter Cascarelli)
Hearings on Organized Crime, "Twenty-five Years After Valachi," 1988 (Testimony of Angelo A. Lonardo)

United States District Court for the Western
District of Missouri:

U.S. vs. Carl DeLuna et al. (Testimony of Angelo A. Lonardo)

STATE GOVERNMENT DOCUMENTS

Ohio Organized Crime Investigations Commission 1993 Status Report

Pennsylvania Crime Commission, 1976, 1992 reports

Attorney General -State of California, Organized Crime Reports to the California Legislature

Cuyahoga County Common Pleas Court:

Greene murder conspiracy case numbers 036324 (Testimony of Raymond Ferritto), 038130 and 042044.

LOCAL GOVERNMENT DOCUMENTS

Akron, Ohio Police Department, Report of Missing Person/Possible Homicide, Leo Moceri, Sep. 1976

Austintown Township, Ohio Police Department. Homicide report: John Conte

Bakerfield, California Coroner's Office, Report of Air Crash death: Kenneth Burnstine

Cleveland Heights, Ohio Police Department, File A42046, Bombing death of Arthur Snepeger

Euclid, Ohio Police Department, Bombing death report of Enos Crnic

Lyndhurst, Ohio Police Department, Homicide report of Daniel J. Greene

Warrensville Heights, Ohio Police Department, Homicide Report of Carmen Semenoro

Index

Rick Porrello is chief of a suburban Cleveland police department. He is author of *The Rise and Fall of the Cleveland Mafia—Corn Sugar and Blood* (Barricade Books, 1995) and *Superthief—A Master Burglar, the Mafia and the Biggest Bank Heist in U.S. History* (Next Hat Press, 2006), winner of a *Foreword Magazine* True Crime award. Porrello began writing his first book during research into the murders of his grandfather and three uncles, Mafia leaders killed in Prohibition-era violence. He is an accomplished jazz drummer having spent three years traveling worldwide with the late, great Sammy Davis Jr.

Visit

RickPorrello.com